June 26, 1974

To Paul
With love, Jean

THE TWELVE
ÆPOSTLES

Ronald Brownrigg

THE TWELVE APOSTLES

Weidenfeld and Nicolson
London

To the people of the parish of
St Mary the Virgin, Blechingley,
with many thanks
for thirteen years' good company

Designed by Rod Josey
for Weidenfeld and Nicolson Ltd
Filmset by Keyspools Ltd, Golborne, Lancs
Printed in Great Britain

ISBN 0297 76732 1

Contents

Foreword

'God considered their works, how they sought him with a perfect heart, and he raised up for them a Teacher of Righteousness to direct them in the way of his heart.' So reads a fragmentary manuscript of the Rule of the Community of the settlement at Qumran, now thought to have been an Essene monastery, in which were written the Dead Sea Scrolls.

This Teacher of Righteousness, in spite of cruel persecution by the high priest(s) of his day, continued to teach his disciples how they could play their part in God's plan of salvation. He gathered round him a 'Council of Twelve', from whom he chose an inner circle of three or so closer companions. The wider community attracted by his teaching and leadership were called the 'Many', who gathered morning and evening for prayer in their Assembly Hall facing Jerusalem. Each Sabbath they shared a ritual meal of bread and wine. On festivals they held a 'love banquet' in preparation for the Last Day, when the Messiah would come to conquer the world and invite the faithful to his triumphal feast.

The familiar pattern of the teacher and his school of disciples was to re-appear a century later, heralded by a desert prophet whose name 'the Baptizer' reflected the initiation rituals of the water channel at Qumran. For Jesus of Nazareth, as for the teacher at Qumran, the group of twelve personal disciples and founder-members was essential to his purpose. Despite the obvious symbolism of the figure twelve, as representative of the tribes of Israel, there is no doubt of the reality of the twelve as part of the historical ministry of Jesus. Even though the various lists of the twelve may appear not to be reconcilable, their authority was clearly recognized in the life of the Christian Church.

It is impossible to overestimate the importance of the twelve for the early Church, or the reverence in which they were held. The twelve were symbolic of the New Israel. As Moses surrounded by the elders and people of Israel gave the Law on the Mount of God, so Jesus surrounded by the twelve and the crowds gave the Law in the Sermon on the Mount. One of the most

Looking east from the escarpment of the Judaean wilderness, through the cleft of Wadi Qumran, the Essene settlement is seen on a plateau to the left.

Scroll jars, which contained the rolled linen and parchment manuscripts, such as were discovered by the Arab goat-boy, Muhammad Adib, in the spring of 1947.

The second Isaiah scroll, before its unfolding, showing how it fitted into its scroll jar.

respected works that did not find acceptance in the canon was the early second-century document called the *Didache*, or Teaching, of the twelve. Nevertheless, as at Qumran, there was an inner circle to be noted in all four Gospels which consisted of Peter, James and John, and on one occasion of Andrew. After the failure of Judas, the number was made up to twelve by the enrolment of a substitute apostle, Matthias, from among those who had been in the company of disciples from the beginning. After the execution of James, the son of Zebedee, however, the number was not again made up to twelve.

This book is concerned with the original twelve and with the substitute, Matthias. There are, however, scholars who see in Paul 'the Apostle to the Gentiles' the last of the twelve and who regard the replacement as having been unnecessary.

High up on the Mount of Olives, below the ancient Constantinian basilica of the Eleona, is a vast cave. This cave early tradition links with a meeting of the twelve to 'parcel out' amongst themselves the known world into twelve areas of mission, each allocated to one of their number. Such a legend accords with the apostolic romances to be found in a group of five Acts of Apostles incorporated into the apocryphal New Testament. There, the Acts of John, Paul, Peter, Andrew and Thomas – as also of the others – form a rhapsody of missionary adventure, however naive, fanciful and unhistorical. The contents of the apocryphal Acts are of little more than legendary value and, as such, are obviously unacceptable within the New Testament canon. The Acts of Paul, for instance, bear no relation to the actions of Paul as recorded in the Acts of the Apostles. Yet, the apocryphal Acts probably reflect the reputations of the different members of the twelve, circulating in the first centuries of the Christian Church. Such material has therefore to be included, but under the clear label of legendary or apocryphal, that is, rejected as manifestly unreliable.

All of the twelve were Jews, who must have accepted Jesus's proclaimed purpose: 'I was sent only to the lost sheep of the house of Israel' (Matt. 15:24). There is little evidence within the New Testament of much specific activity outside Israel by members of the twelve. By the baptism of Cornelius, Peter accepted in principle the universality of the Christian gospel; he also visited the early missionary headquarters at Antioch. Elsewhere in the Acts of the Apostles, however, the only missionary apostle specifically mentioned is Paul, who was assisted by Barnabas and countless Christians from the eastern Mediterranean. We are therefore faced with the questions: when did the original twelve apostles begin their travels? When did the mission to Israel extend to the nations?

Although it is not possible to offer scriptural evidence of the travels of any one of the original twelve, apart from Peter, certain facts may be inferred from the canonical New Testament, in addition to a great deal of fiction from the apocryphal writings. When Paul visited Jerusalem at the end of his three-year retreat following his conversion (Gal. 1:18–19), he spent a fortnight with Peter, but never met any of the other apostles. Where were they? The Apostolic Council at Jerusalem appears to have been in the habit of dispatching its members on specific missions. Peter and John were sent to Samaria to consolidate the evangelistic success of Philip (Acts 8:14). Judas Barsabbas and Silas were sent to Antioch to convey a decision of the Council (Acts 15:22). It would seem too that Paul used the term 'apostles' more widely and more literally than in reference to the twelve original apostles of Jesus. Judging by the last chapter of the Letter to the Romans, whether it was for the Roman or the Ephesian congregation, Paul had many apostles of his own. These included women such as Phoebe the deaconess, and Prisca the

An engraving of Moses presenting the Tablets of the Law to the people of Israel, at the foot of Mount Sinai.

wife of Aquila, besides such men as Timothy, Titus and Silvanus. Indeed, Paul's correspondence gives the impression of considerable coming and going both of true and false apostles among his Mediterranean congregations, though whether these included any of the twelve is open to question.

It would seem that the earliest mission of the infant Church was to Israel. In Mark's Gospel, the first to be circulated – in the year 64 or 65 – there is

Jesus giving the Sermon on the Mount to his Twelve Apostles, a painting by Fra. Giovanni in the Museum of St Mark at Florence.

little reference to a universal commission, even though this Gospel enshrines the reminiscences of Peter himself. The mission to Israel appears to cease with the decamping of the headquarters of the Judaeo–Christian Church to Pella, followed by the destruction of Jerusalem in the year 70 and the consequent diaspora. The post-70 writings of Matthew and Luke make a point of a universal commission to 'all nations' and to 'the end of the earth' (Matt. 28:19; Acts 1:8). It is not possible to know who of the twelve, other than Peter and perhaps John, followed the pioneering example of Paul.

Christians today may well wish to link the twelve with the development of Christianity in specific parts of the world, as did Christians of the second and third centuries within the apocryphal Acts of Apostles. All that can be done with honesty is to record the geographical progress of the Gospel, to note which apostle has been the patron saint and inspiration to the Christian community in a particular part of the world, and to present their fascinating but fanciful traditions.

The primary task of this book is to follow the fortunes of each member of the twelve, to sketch in each individual's character so far as the canonical and apocryphal New Testament material and early ecclesiastical histories would seem to reveal it. To this end, the intention is to study the scriptural evidence of what is *known*, then what may be *detected* or *surmised* of the identification, relationships and function of each apostle, and finally what may be *derived* from such legendary and apocryphal material as is relevant. On the canvas of the Roman-ruled world of the first century, against a background of the brief Galilean ministry, based on their provincial headquarters at Capernaum, it is hoped that their collective and individual portraits will stand out in historical and scriptural perspective.

Part I
THE MESSIANIC COMMUNITY

Out of Zion, the perfection of beauty,
   God shines forth.
Our God comes, he does not keep silence,
   before him is a devouring fire,
   round about him a mighty tempest.
He calls to the heavens above
   and to the earth, that he may judge
   his people:
'Gather to me my faithful ones,
   who made a covenant with me by
   sacrifice!'
The heavens declare his righteousness,
   for God himself is judge!
                     (Psalm 50:2–6)

1 Salvation is from the Jews*

It was the year 26, the year of Pontius Pilate's appointment as Roman pro-curator of Judaea. Three years later he was officially responsible for the con-demnation and crucifixion of a certain Jewish rabbi of about his own age, on a charge of sedition. This young Roman aristocrat, Pontius 'the pike-man', was proud, hot-tempered and obstinate, capable of childish behaviour when his will was crossed, and as military-minded as his name suggests. His appointment lasted a decade, before he was recalled to Rome and his career terminated by banishment in disgrace to Gaul. Although, strangely enough, the Abyssinian Church has made a saint of him, the Apostles' and Nicene Creeds have branded him throughout the Christian world by referring to that certain Jewish rabbi as 'crucified also for us under Pontius Pilate'.

It was in the following year, AD 27, that a cousin of this same Jewish rabbi who was to be crucified appeared out of the Judaean wilderness to herald the coming of the Messiah and to proclaim the baptism of repentance for the forgiveness of sins. The rugged wilderness was prone to the hot desert wind, the earthquake rift and the fire of forked lightning and even of volcanic action. The deserted and silent wilderness was the traditional source of the 'still small voice' of inspiration, and the asceticism of John and his sudden emergence upon the national scene was in the tradition of Elijah and the primitive prophets of the Old Testament.

Perhaps John had been associated with the Essenes, who pursued the ideals of purity and holiness in the isolation of the desert. Certainly he was influenced by their practices, particularly by their ritual washings and cleansings, not to mention their formation of a company of disciples seeking to 'fly from the retribution that is coming', as he put it. John, however, must not be confused with such ecclesiastical schism or sectarianism. His kind of asceticism was that of the 'Nazarites', a word whose primary meaning implies separation and consecration to a life-long vow. The outward appearance of John's devotion must have been clear for all to see: his long uncut hair, his primitive diet and his total abstinence from the fruit of the vine.

*From the words of Jesus to the woman of Samaria (John 4:22).

A painting of John the Baptist in the wilderness, by Romano.

The single figure on a donkey emerging from the valley of the Jordan and dwarfed by the desert wilderness, epitomises the courageous individuality of the Baptist.

Inspired by John's own example and his call for repentance, together with a return to a greater simplicity of life, and roused by his strident proclamation of the coming of the Messianic kingdom, the crowds gathered from all over Judaea and Samaria. In what may rightly be called 'a great religious revival' people of all strata of society flocked down through the wilderness to be baptized by John at the fords of the Jordan. The strength and power of this religious movement is reflected in the fact that, twenty years later, there were still disciples of John to be found in Alexandria and Ephesus.

The directness and simplicity of his message struck home: 'You brood of vipers! Who warned you to flee from the wrath to come? Bear fruits that befit repentance, and do not begin to say to yourselves, "We have Abraham as our father"; for I tell you, God is able from these stones to raise up children to Abraham. Even now the axe is laid to the root of the trees; every tree therefore that does not bear good fruit is cut down and thrown into the fire.' And the multitudes asked him, 'What then shall we do?' And he answered them, 'He who has two coats, let him share with him who has none; and he who has food, let him do likewise.' Tax collectors also came to be baptized, and said to him, 'Teacher, what shall we do?' And he said to them, 'Collect no more than is appointed you.' Soldiers also asked him, 'And we, what shall we do?' And he said to them, 'Rob no one by violence or by false accusation, and be content with your wages' (Luke 3: 7–14). That

The Baptism of Christ, by Verocchio, in the Uffizi Gallery, Florence. The hands of the Father release the Spirit as a dove upon his Son.

message, however, clearly pointed to the imminent arrival of 'one who is to come'. 'I baptize you with water; but he who is mightier than I is coming, the thong of whose sandals I am not worthy to untie; he will baptize you with the Holy Spirit and with fire. His winnowing fork is in his hand, to clear his threshing floor, and to gather the wheat into his granary, but the chaff he will burn with unquenchable fire' (Luke 3: 16–17).

Among the disciples and companions of John, down by the river Jordan, there was a group from Galilee, which included his cousin Jesus of Nazareth. Jesus clearly associated himself with the revivalist campaign of the Baptist by insisting on himself being baptized by John. The story of his baptism, as the Gospel of Mark describes it, is much more than an indication of the acceptance by Jesus of the message of John. It is an account of a personal experience of Jesus, a revelation to him both of his Messiahship and of the method of his Messiahship. 'And when he came up out of the water, immediately he saw the heavens opened and the Spirit descending upon him like a dove; and a voice came from heaven, "Thou art my beloved Son; with thee I am well pleased"' (Mark 1:10–11). Jesus must have told this story

The upper reaches of the River Jordan.

This Arab felaheen separates the grain from the chaff, by lifting the corn into the wind with his winnowing fork – 'purging the threshing floor'.

himself and cannot have failed to point out that the words of the voice were quoted from the Psalms and the Book of Isaiah. The first words came from Psalm 2, generally believed to refer to the King Messiah: 'He said to me, "You are my son".' The other words of the voice came from the Suffering Servant passages of the Book of Isaiah, which Jesus repeatedly quoted during his ministry: 'Behold my servant, whom I uphold, my chosen, in whom my soul delights' (Isa. 42:1).

At his baptism, Jesus became awakened to and convinced of his Sonship, as the Messiah of his people. He also became supremely aware of the cost in suffering that his calling would demand from him. The immediate effect of this experience was to drive him into the wilderness to face the consequences of this new realization. From that moment, as Peter recorded in his speech to Cornelius, 'God anointed Jesus of Nazareth with the Holy Spirit and with power' (Acts 10: 38).

Though some suggest that this was a subjective experience of Jesus alone, the Fourth Gospel insists that John the Baptist was also aware of the descent of the Spirit upon Jesus, who was thus clearly to be identified as the 'Coming One' who shall baptize with the Holy Spirit of God. 'After me comes a man who ranks before me, for he was before me. I myself did not

know him; but for this I came baptizing with water, that he might be revealed to Israel.' And John bore witness, 'I saw the Spirit descend as a dove from heaven, and it remained on him. I myself did not know him; but he who sent me to baptize with water said to me, "He on whom you see the Spirit descend and remain, this is he who baptizes with the Holy Spirit." And I have seen and have borne witness that this is the Son of God' (John 1:30–34).

The latest of the canonical Gospels, that of John, relates that the discipleship of Jesus's first followers dated from this event, when John the Baptist, surrounded by his own disciples, virtually withdrew, leaving them to form the core of Jesus's own band of followers. For a time, the Fourth Gospel indicates, the ministry of the two men was simultaneous until Jesus attracted the greater following, seemingly with John's own encouragement. For, when John's disciples questioned him: 'Rabbi, he who was with you beyond the Jordan, to whom you bore witness, here he is, baptizing, and all are going to him,' John answered, 'No one can receive anything except what is given him from heaven. You yourselves bear me witness, that I said, I am not the Christ, but I have been sent before him. He who has the bride is the bridegroom; the friend of the bridegroom, who stands and hears him, rejoices greatly at the bridegroom's voice; therefore this joy of mine is now full. He must increase, but I must decrease' (John 3:26–30).

The earlier Gospels of Mark and Matthew imply that the public ministry of Jesus did not begin until after the imprisonment of John the Baptist – an event which, the Jewish historian Josephus says, shocked the people. Mark tells the story retrospectively of how John was imprisoned by Herod Antipas for denouncing Herod's marriage with Herodias, his brother Philip's wife. John's courage rivalled that of the prophet Elijah in his denunciation of Ahab and Jezebel. Biblical prophecy depends on the human acceptance of God's terms for its fulfilment. Since John's message was to be accepted – which generally it was – then his ministry became that foretold in the name of Elijah. Both of them were forerunners, and both of them concentrated their courage on the spot where it could witness most dramatically for righteousness – the royal palace.

When in prison, John sent his disciples to Jesus with the question, 'Are you He who is to come?' His question may have indicated his doubt, but more likely his hope that he was to have a successor and that he had not been a failure after all. Jesus's answer, mentioning his performance of the works predicted for the Messiah, should have reassured him. Matthew and Mark describe John's execution in Galilee, at Herod's command, to fulfil a rash promise to Herodias's daughter, Salome. This took place, according to Josephus, in Herod's fortress of Machaerus, an isolated Hasmonean outpost east of the Dead Sea. Mark's Gospel took the baptism of Jesus by John as its historical starting point, but showed that Jesus did not launch his campaign in Galilee until after his cousin's execution. It was indeed against

ABOVE The Baptist witnesses to his own disciples, John and Andrew, the identity of Jesus as the 'Lamb of God'. Mosaic within 6th-century Kariye Camii, Istanbul.

BELOW John in Prison, from the Baptistery, Florence, is flanked by soldiers in medieval armour. The scale of the Baptist's figure dwarfs that of his guards.

The beheading of John the Baptist, at the whim of Salome and the order of Herod Antipas. Painting by Caravaggio, in the Cathedral of St John, Malta.

the background of this frightening event that Jesus conducted his own brief ministry.

Just how long Jesus remained in the company of John and his disciples may never be known, but he probably returned to Galilee in the spring of the year 28. The following summer he spent preaching and teaching in the local synagogues on the theme of 'the kingdom of God', as well as performing many new acts of healing on those who believed. He also called the first five, if not all, of his twelve disciples.

He declared that: 'The time is fulfilled, and the kingdom of God is at hand' (Mark 1:15). From the beginning of their life as a nation, the Israelites had believed themselves to be under the rule of God. During their history, before and after their exile in Babylon, they came to think of the kingdom of God as including all nations, although the other nations did not

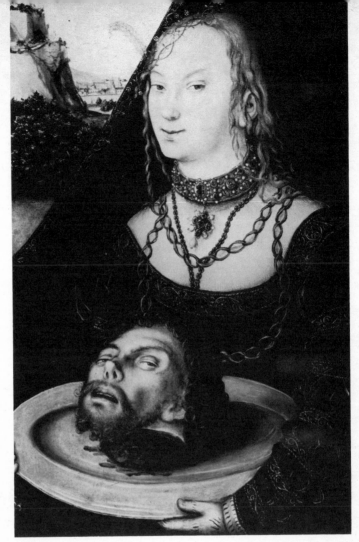

Salome, daughter of Herodias, holding the head of the Baptist 'in a charger', the reward of her dancing. Painting by Lucas Cranach.

acknowledge the rule of God. Over his own people God was the supreme ruler; but he was opposed by the other nations and this opposition would in the end be overcome. During and after the exile of the Jews in Babylon, the recovery of the independence of Israel was expected to be achieved under a prince of David's line, the Anointed of the Lord or the Messiah. Then God would reign in the whole world. The prophets of Israel had foretold a day of judgement and purging by suffering which would precede and usher in the universal rule of God. When the Jews were in the grip of alien occupation and persecution, under the empires of Babylon, Persia, Greece and Rome, they hoped for the triumph of the kingdom or empire of God, after the fall of all these empires, as the result of a supernatural intervention in human history. The writers of the Book of Daniel and the Book of Enoch foretold a 'Son of God' descending through the clouds to establish the kingdom of

God in the future, at the end of the period in which the world is dominated by the 'Beasts' which are the imperial powers. This hope of supernatural deliverance is called 'apocalyptic', as it meant that God would reveal or unveil his purpose for his people.

The arrival of Jesus in Galilee, declaring that 'the time is fulfilled, and the kingdom of God is at hand' (Mark 1:15), had a tremendous impact on the simple people and drew all of them, including the Scribes and Pharisees and Zealots, coming from all directions, to hear his message. Jesus believed in the present sovereignty of God and the future universal manifestation of that sovereignty. But he also insisted that the power of the kingdom of God was already at work in the world, through his own coming. Jesus declared that the rule of God comes here and now, insofar as it is acknowledged, and becomes a reality at once to those who accept it. 'But if it is by the Spirit of God that I cast out demons, then the Kingdom of God has come upon you' (Matt. 12:28). 'But blessed are your eyes, for they see, and your ears, for they hear. Truly, I say to you, many prophets and righteous men longed to see what you see, and did not see it, and to hear what you hear, and did not hear it' (Matt. 13:16–17). At Nazareth Jesus read a passage from the Book of Isaiah, concerning the Messiah: 'The Spirit of the Lord is upon me, because the Lord has anointed me to bring good tidings to the afflicted; he has sent me to bind up the broken-hearted, to proclaim liberty to the captives, and the opening of the prison to those who are bound: to proclaim the year of the Lord's favour' (Isa. 61:1–2). (Cf. Luke 4:18–19: 'Because he has anointed me to preach good news to the poor. He has sent me to proclaim release to the captives and recovering of sight to the blind, to set at liberty those who are oppressed, to proclaim the acceptable year of the Lord.') He then rolled up the scroll and declared: 'Today has this scripture been fulfilled in your hearing' (Luke 4:21). When the Pharisees asked him to tell them when the kingdom of God would come, he replied, 'Behold, the kingdom of God is in the midst of you' (Luke 17:21).

Even the miracles of Jesus were interpreted as signs of the coming of the kingdom of God. In his time there was no dispute about the possibility of miracles and the reality of supernatural power was assumed. Two Greek words sometimes translated by the word 'miracle' appear in one sentence of a speech by Peter in Jerusalem, on the feast of Pentecost following the death and Resurrection of Jesus. 'Jesus of Nazareth, a man attested to you by God with mighty works [Greek *dynameis*] and portents and signs [Greek *semeia*] which God did through him, as you yourselves know,' is the subject of Peter's speech. The first word used, *dynameis*, meant 'acts of power'; the word translated as 'signs' (*semeia*) alluded to the meanings of these acts of power. In modern times miracles are events thought to be beyond the known power of natural causes and therefore attributed to the supernatural by those who believe in it. In the days of Jesus, miracles were also signs of divine power of which the true importance lay in what they might signify. The parables of Jesus were homespun stories of real life with an inner spiritual meaning which could be perceived only by those whose listening and thinking were in tune with the mind of the teacher. The miracles of Jesus seem to have been acted parables; they and the stories about them have a meaning which could not be grasped except by those who believed in Jesus. According to the Gospels the Pharisees still asked Jesus for a sign, after seeing all his miracles. Jesus said to his disciples, 'To you it has been given to know the secrets of the kingdom of heaven, but to them it has not been given' (Matt. 13:11). The writer of the Gospel of Matthew adds, as a comment, a quotation from the Book of Isaiah: 'You shall indeed hear but never understand, and you shall indeed see but never perceive. For this people's heart has grown dull, and their ears are heavy of hearing, and their eyes they have closed, lest they should perceive with their eyes, and hear with their ears, and understand with their heart, and turn for me to heal them' (Matt. 13:14–15; cf. Isa. 6:9–10). Without faith in Jesus in the minds and hearts of the eye-witnesses, the miracles of Jesus were not an effective means of showing his identity as the Messiah.

The crowds gathered, as they had done to John the Baptist, and the people came not only from Judaea and Galilee, Tyre and Sidon over the border, but from the Decapolis beyond the Jordan. The source of his power was his extraordinary personality and authority, revealed in both his teaching and his healing. Just as John had attracted the representatives of the Scribes and Pharisees, so the religious authorities in Jerusalem sent their delegations to assess the spiritual integrity of Jesus. They were fearful of the massive response of the people and of the scale that the movement was assuming. It was perhaps his proclamation of the kingdom of God and his acts of both healing and forgiveness that most strongly conflicted with the legalistic Pharisaism of his day. The religious authorities were simply unable to accept the source of his power as inspired by God and declared that it must be diabolic. Therefore their reports condemned him as another false, in fact a blasphemous, claimant to Messiahship. Their assessment of him as a magician who deceived the people was later reflected in the Mishnah.

Retrospective if not contemporary Christian opinion has naturally justified his claims, has seen in his acts of healing and exorcism, and indeed in all his miracles, the hallmark of his Messiahship. Similarly his ministry of forgiveness has been justified as part of his ministry of healing the whole of a man. Thus Jesus, by curing the body, showed his power to heal the spirit. As the diseases of body and spirit were thought to be interdependent, those who had faith in Jesus believed him to have power over the bodies and spirits of men. When Jesus healed the paralytic who was carried to him at Capernaum, seeing the patient on a pallet he said, 'My son, your sins are forgiven.' The scribes then accused him of blasphemy, saying: 'Who can forgive sins, but God alone?' Jesus asked them, 'Which is easier, to say to the paralytic, "Your sins are forgiven", or to say, "Rise, take up your pallet and walk"? But that you may know that the Son of Man has authority on earth to forgive sins', Jesus then said to the paralytic, 'I say to you, rise, take up your pallet and go home' (Mark 2 : 5–11).

Christian scholars have pointed to Messianic prophecies and parallels, such as Isaiah, chapter 61, indicating that the Messiah's coming would be accompanied by the healing of disease and the liberation of men from the power of evil. Mental illness, like physical illness, was regarded as spiritual in origin. It was described as the possession of a person who was ill by evil spirits and demons. The exorcists of the time of Jesus employed magical formulas and spells of a religious character. Jesus cast out demons by his own authority, ordering them to go out of the person possessed by them. This power was believed to demonstrate his Messiahship. 'If it is by the finger of God that I cast out demons, then the kingdom of God is come upon you,' he said in an argument with his opponent (Luke 11 : 20). The demons are represented as recognizing his Messianic power, as they cry out with a loud voice, 'What have you to do with us, O Son of God? Have you come here to torment us before the time?' (Matt. 8 : 29). On another occasion the evil spirit shouts, 'I know who you are, [the] Holy One of God' (Mark 1 : 24).

Within this first year of crowded activity throughout the synagogues and villages of Galilee, the opposition of the establishment steadily mounted. He and his disciples appear to have been forced to retire to the lakeside and he no longer seems to have had access to the synagogue pulpits, except perhaps at his 'home town', Capernaum. It is at this time, possibly, that he and his disciples travelled to and fro across the lake, followed by the crowd moving along the north shore. They even followed him up into the hills and into open country or deserted places, five thousand at a time. By the lakeside, particularly along the north coast, the crowds packed the little bays which formed natural auditoria with the hills rising from the water's edge, and the voice of Jesus, sitting in Peter's boat, would be carried up the hillsides and round the bay impelled by the natural sounding board of the lake water (Mark 4).

The disciples no doubt served a fairly rigorous apprenticeship during Jesus's itinerant ministry. His own upbringing in the cosmopolitan market township of Nazareth, so near the great trade route from Damascus to Egypt, must have been a rough and ready schooling for his own public life of open-air preaching and the heckling of his opponents. The twelve graduated successfully after their preliminary training when Jesus commissioned them by pairs, both to preach and to heal. 'And he called to him his twelve disciples and gave them authority over unclean spirits, to cast them out, and to heal every disease and every infirmity. These twelve Jesus sent out, charging them, "Go nowhere among the Gentiles, and enter no town of the Samari-

The view from the hilltop at Nazareth looking down to the Plain of Esdraelon, through which passed the ancient trade route, 'Via Maris'.

tans, but go rather to the lost sheep of the house of Israel. And preach as you go, saying, 'The kingdom of heaven is at hand.' Heal the sick, raise the dead, cleanse lepers, cast out demons. You received without pay, give without pay. Take no gold, nor silver, nor copper in your belts, no bag for your journey, nor two tunics, nor sandals, nor a staff; for the labourer deserves his food. And whatever town or village you enter, find out who is worthy in it, and stay with him until you depart. As you enter the house, salute it. And if the house is worthy, let your peace come upon it; but if it is not worthy, let your peace return to you. And if any one will not receive you or listen to your words, shake off the dust from your feet as you leave that house or town'' (Matt. 10:1, 5–14).

The twelve were forbidden to go to any but to 'the lost sheep of the house of Israel'. Their instructions were very specific and they were almost identical to those given to the 'seventy others' to be found in Luke's Gospel (10:1–11). The two figures, 'twelve' and 'seventy', are of particular significance, the twelve as before mentioned, signifying each of the tribes of the 'house of Israel', the seventy signifying the peoples or languages of the whole world. In the Targum of Jonathan on the text Gen. 11:7, the building of the Tower of Babel, is this commentary: 'The Lord said to the seventy angels who stood before him, Come now, let us go down and there confound their tongues, that no man may understand the tongue of his neighbour. And the Word of the Lord was revealed against that city, and with him seventy angels, corresponding to the seventy people.'

An illustration from the
Bedford *Book of Hours*
showing the angels
scattering the builders of
the Tower of Babel.

Thus, the number of the second apostolate of the 'seventy others' corresponded to the spiritual company of angels at Babel. This second apostolate was to constitute an earthly band of missionaries to the world. The
duplication of their briefing, to the seventy as well as to the twelve, is to be
found only in Luke's Gospel, however, the only Gospel written by a Gentile.
It is also in harmony with the universalist presentation of this particular
Gospel and therefore open to some suspicion. This explanation was, however, known and accepted by some of the early Church Fathers, including
Cyril of Alexandria. 'Christ meant', according to Cyril, 'to show by his
expansion of the twelve into the seventy, that he was driving the nations as
well as Israel into his great net.' Nevertheless, of these two accounts, of the
primitive mission of the twelve and that of the seventy others, it is the
former and *non*-universalist account which is the original and the second
which is the modification. The earliest known account of the apostolate is
the one which offers twelve persons commissioned to the twelve tribes of
Israel.

The Call of Peter and Andrew, a 6th-century mosaic in St Apollinare Nuovo, Ravenna. Andrew (dark hair) rows the dinghy, while Peter (light hair, round beard) draws the net.

A rabbi and his disciples, today.

2 The Synagogue of the Twelve

'Jesus the Christ was sent by God. Thus Christ is from God, and the apostles from Christ. He and they came into being in harmony from the will of God.' So wrote Clement, bishop of Rome, at the turn of the first century. Who were the apostles who founded the seminary of God's word, the college of disciples, who were to become the foundation-stones of the Christian Church? Who were the twelve men of whom John the Divine in his apocalyptic visions on Patmos wrote, 'The wall of the city had twelve foundations, and on them the twelve names of the twelve apostles of the Lamb'? (Rev. 21:14).

The core of the Qumrani community was a council of twelve laymen and an inner circle of three priests. The *minyan* or *quorum* for public prayer and the reading of the Law or Prophets within the synagogue was ten Jewish males above the age of thirteen years. The Talmud (Ber. 6:a) infers the presence of God only when sufficient men are present for a particular purpose. Thus the Rabbi Adda asks: 'How do you know that if ten men pray together . . . that if three are sitting as a court of judges . . . the divine presence is with them?' Abba Benjamin answers: 'For it saith that God stands in the congregation of God.' The words 'synagogue' (from the Greek) and 'congregation' (from the Latin) are synonymous, meaning 'gathered'. The word 'synagogue', like 'church', has the double meaning of both the people and the place. Thus the first Christian synagogue consisted of the twelve and of the Upper Room (in the house of Mary the mother of Mark), which was for long held to be the scene of the Last Supper and of the descent of the Spirit at Pentecost. This room was destined to become the first headquarters of the Jerusalem Church.

The group of twelve had its roots deep in the Old Testament. Judaism preserved and interpreted the Old Testament through the institution of the rabbi and his disciples. Although God himself was the primary teacher of the Law, human teachers could be his agents or instruments. The rabbi could become both the reader and the interpreter of God's will for each in-

The Legend of St Andrew, by Bartolemneo di Giovanni. Maximilla, wife of Aegeates, pro-consul of Achaia, is healed and converted despite her husband's opposition.

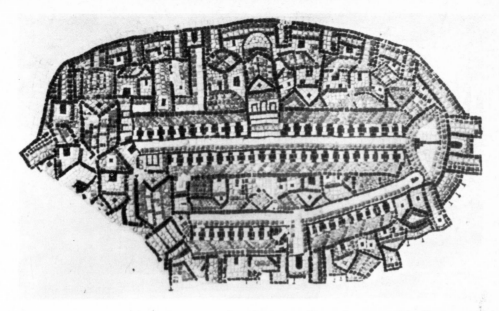

The city of Jerusalem from the centre of a 6th-century Byzantine map of the Eastern Mediterranean, discovered in 1890. The Holy Sepulchre is visible in the centre.

dividual Israelite. It was the rabbi's vocation to teach the ordering of rela-tionships towards both God and man. Students who themselves aspired to become rabbis served an apprenticeship to a rabbi of their own choice. The disciple lived in close community with his adopted teacher, looking after his practical and domestic needs, and at the same time receiving instruction in the Law and its interpretation, in order to carry out all the Law's demands in his own life. Later the rabbinic student would in turn become a rabbi with his own disciples, to pass on this teaching to others and so help to build up the Holy People awaiting the Messianic salvation.

The Law was the bond which united disciples and rabbi. Both were dedicated to its service and the ideal that all Israelites should keep the Law. Some rabbis looked to the actual time of the Messiah as a time of study of the Law, under the teaching and interpretation of the Messiah himself.

In the Gospels, Jesus is called 'rabbi' forty-one times and the twelve are called disciples more than one hundred and eighty times. Jesus and his methods of teaching had many rabbinic characteristics. He taught in the synagogues on the Sabbath. He taught in parables, a usual form of school instruction. He was respected for his teaching. He and his group were served and sometimes financed by a group of women acquaintances. He did not, however, conform to the usual rabbinic pattern. His teaching was not con-fined to the synagogue, but often took place in the open air by the lakeside or in the villages. His Galilean following included a wide variety: women, sinners and tax-collectors. There was no exclusiveness about Jesus or his company of disciples. He could never be mistaken for just another rabbi.

There were some peculiar features of Jesus's rabbi-disciple relationship. Unlike other groups it was he, the rabbi, who chose and called his pupils; and they followed him immediately. The initiative of selection was his, nor did they appear to aspire to graduate as rabbis themselves. In their group there was only to be one 'Master'. Jesus told them, 'But you are not to be called rabbi, for you have one teacher, and you are all brethren. And call no man your father on earth, for you have one Father, who is in heaven. Neither be called masters, for you have one master, the Christ. He who is greatest among you shall be your servant' (Matt. 23:8–11).

The fundamental difference between the disciples of Jesus and those of Judaism was in the loyalties required of them. Most circles of rabbis and pupils were bound by a mutual dependence upon the Law and their zeal to interpret it and to promote its observance. The disciples of Jesus were bound by a direct loyalty to his own person. For he proclaimed that the kingdom of the rule of God had arrived with his own coming. He demanded of his followers a change of heart based on his own interpretation and adaptation of the Law. Over and over again he declared, as in the Sermon on the Mount, 'You have heard what was said to them of old, but *I* say unto you . . .'; consequently the twelve formed the nucleus of a community round the person of Jesus, rather than bound by a mutual study of the Law.

Their community of life together was intended to prepare them for their future ministry. *The* twelve were a well-recognized and specific group within his wider following, whose relationship to Jesus is clearly expressed, particularly in certain passages of the Fourth Gospel. 'If you continue in my word, you are truly my disciples' (8:31). The blind man whose sight was restored asked the Pharisees whether they too wanted to become disciples of Jesus. They answered him curtly: 'You are his disciple, but we are disciples of Moses. We know that God has spoken to Moses, but as for this man, we do not know where he comes from' (9:28–29). Jesus's disciples were to be closely knit by their love and loyalty, not only to him but to each other: 'By this all men will know that you are my disciples, if you have love for one another' (13:35). Nevertheless, their primary loyalty remains to the person and teaching of Jesus himself: 'If you abide in me and my words abide in you . . . by this my Father is glorified, that you bear much fruit, and so prove to be my disciples' (15:7–8).

'*The* twelve', then, were a well-recognized and distinct group. They formed a collective entity rather than a number of individuals, just as Israel had been a twelve-tribe people, a confederacy surrounding a common sanctuary. Israel's very name originated from Jacob, the father of the twelve patriarchs. As the confederacy of the twelve tribes was based on Israel's consciousness of their covenant relationship to God, the twelve were also bound by a bond of loyalty and obedience to their rabbi, Jesus. They could

Christ healing the blind man, a painting by Duccio di Buoninsegna.

not but be aware of the historical significance of their number, as equivalent to that of the tribes. They would remember that the altar of covenant sacrifice on Sinai had been built of twelve pillars 'according to the twelve tribes of Israel' (Exod. 24:4). They would remember Joshua's memorial at Gilgal of thanksgiving for the entry into Canaan: 'Then Joshua called the twelve men from the people of Israel, whom he had appointed, a man from each tribe; and Joshua said to them, "Pass on before the ark of the Lord your God into the midst of the Jordan, and take up each of you a stone upon his shoulder, according to the tribes of the people of Israel, that this may be a sign among you, when your children ask in time to come, 'What do those stones mean to you?' ... So these stones shall be to the people of Israel a memorial for ever"' (Josh. 4:4–6, 7).

Though the kingdom and tribes were later divided, their restored unity

The cure of the paralytic, from the tabernacle of a Sistine chapel in the Vatican Grotto.

was always the dream of the great prophets. In the Servant Songs of the second Isaiah (49:6) it is the destiny of the Messianic figure of the Servant 'to raise up the tribes of Jacob and to restore the preserved of Israel'. Similarly Ezekiel is commanded to demonstrate the future union of the kingdoms by the visual aid of two sticks. 'Behold, I am about to take the stick of Joseph (which is in the hand of Ephraim) and the tribes of Israel associated with him; and I will join it with the stick of Judah, and make them one stick, that they may be one in my hand' (Ezek. 37:19).

There is no doubt that the twelvefold structure of both the Qumran hierarchy and of Jesus's followers was inspired by the twelve-tribe concept of Israel and also by hopes of a Messianic restoration of its unity. An Essene document, probably belonging to the period immediately before Christ, called 'The Testaments of the Twelve Patriarchs', looked forward to the re-establishment of the twelve tribes in a restored temple. Jesus, by his choice of the twelve, appears to have purposefully linked his community with this contemporary expectation.

As he accommodated his method and teaching to the needs and capacity of his pupils, it was natural that he should establish his Messianic community on this known structure of the twelve. Such a choice would be full of significance for its members, for the very name of 'the twelve' was far more important than the actual name of the group. 'The twelve' signified a reality far more fundamental than any of the individuals who went to make up the number. They represent the corpus of apostolic witness to the Resurrection and identity of Jesus. Their spokesman, Simon Peter, quoted the Psalms of David, who 'foresaw and spoke of the Resurrection of the Christ. . . . This Jesus God raised up, and of that we all are witnesses. Let the house of Israel therefore know assuredly that God has made him both Lord and Christ, this Jesus whom you crucified' (Acts 2:32, 36). The twelve were chosen, called, taught and commissioned to be the Messianic community first to the 'lost sheep of the house of Israel' and then to the world at large.

The significance of the number which made up this community should not obscure the infinite care in the selection of each individual member. Jesus appears to have called a number of men from their daily occupations, among them Simon and Andrew from casting a net into the lake, James and John from mending their nets, Matthew from his customs ledger, Philip at the fords of Jordan, Nathaniel from under his fig tree in Cana. It is likely that all of these and more were originally disciples of John the Baptist. There came a time, perhaps as much as a year later, when he needed to select from his many disciples a group of twelve whom he should appoint, empower and commission as his apostles. As was his custom in times of crisis and decision, he left the lakeside and went up into the hills to spend the whole night on his own. The following morning he called his disciples to him, those whom he wanted, and they came. From them he chose the twelve, whom he named 'apostles', to be *with* him; to form his gathered (or synagogue) community. (At this point, each of the three earliest and Synoptic Gospels lists the individual members of the group.) Then Jesus 'came down' and 'went home', presumably to Capernaum.

There are, broadly speaking, two different traditions reflected in the lists of the twelve to be found in Mark's, Matthew's and Luke's Gospels, together with the list of those present at the election of a successor to Judas Iscariot, this last list to be found in the first chapter of the Acts. The priority of Mark's Gospel and his list is now hardly questioned by scholars. This order and identification of each man is closely followed in Matthew's Gospel, except that Matthew pairs off the first two sets of brothers, Simon and Andrew, James and John. Mark on the other hand lists the inner circle of Simon, James and John before mentioning Andrew and the rest. Thus, the Gospels of Mark and Matthew combine to make up one tradition.

The Gospel of Luke and the Acts are successive volumes from the mind and hand of Luke. As their lists refer to different occasions, the Gospel to the selection of the twelve during the ministry, the Acts to the gathering after the Ascension of Jesus, the order is different but the identification is the same. The Gospel of Luke pairs the brothers of Bethsaida together, but otherwise virtually follows Mark's order. The list in the Acts puts the inner circle first, but unlike the other three lists significantly promotes Thomas from eighth to fifth place, as though Thomas rose in importance between the ministry and the Ascension. The part played by Thomas in events after the Resurrection, both in the Upper Room and on the lake, may well account for a change in status. These two Lucan accounts in the Gospel and in the Acts provide the second tradition, while the scattered references by name to only seven apostles within the Fourth Gospel may be said to form a third tradition.

The apparent discrepancies of identity will be discussed in detail within the relevant chapters that follow, but there are only three of these discrepancies. Of these, one may be easily solved by linking the personal name with the patronymic, Nathaniel with Bartholomew. The second is a matter of translation between the Aramaic and the Greek, the equation of Simon the *Cananaean* (Aramaic for 'zealous'), with Simon the 'Zealot', from the Green word *zelotes*. The last involves the linking of a personal with a nickname, or with a variation of his own name. Thus 'Judas, son of James', alias 'Judas, not Iscariot', has been identified with Thaddaeus which could mean in Hebrew 'big-hearted', or might equally be a variation of Theudas, which is just another form of Judas. The following list matches off these three traditions.

MATTHEW/MARK	LUKE/ACTS	JOHN
Simon Peter	Simon Peter	Simon Peter
Andrew	Andrew	Andrew
James	James	'Sons of
John	John	Zebedee'
Philip	Philip	Philip
Bartholomew	Bartholomew	= Nathaniel
Matthew	Matthew	—
Thomas	Thomas	Thomas
James, son of Alphaeus	James, son of Alphaeus	—
Thaddaeus	= Judas, son of James	= Judas, not Iscariot
Simon the Cananaean	= Simon the Zealot	—
Judas Iscariot	Judas Iscariot	Judas, son of Simon, Iscariot

Part 2
THE MEMBERS

As in one body we have many members, and all the members do not have the same function, so we, though many, are one body in Christ, and individually members one of another (Romans 12:4-5).

3 Andrew and Peter, Brothers from Bethsaida

There is a sense in which the twelve could collectively be called 'Brothers of Bethsaida', for *beth-saida* means 'fisher-home' and there were several round the north shore of the Lake of Galilee. All but one of the twelve were Galileans and more than half their number were professional fishermen. At first sight, Galilee would appear to have been a strange choice for the growth of a new religious movement, and a crew of fishermen an even stranger choice for its founder members.

Christians from St Paul onwards have found historical and religious reasons for the 'fullness of time', and the election of that particular people on the oriental fringe of the Roman colonial empire. Indeed the Augustan age, with its wise and peaceful rule, its improved communications and trading facilities, did much to assist the rapid spread of the movement, as did the single *lingua franca* of colloquial Greek in use throughout the Mediterranean world.

Hebrew prophecy had flowered into rich monotheism and universalism: scribal interpretation had reached new depths of perception: under the stimulus of exile and persecution, Jewish spiritual life had developed new convictions of faith and vocation. In successive conquests, Jewish communities with their synagogues had been scattered throughout the near east, each attracting their proselytes and God-fearers. The apostolic missions of this new movement could therefore build upon foundations in scripture, synagogue, apocalyptic and Messianic expectation already well laid among the Jews of the diaspora.

Certainly, the seeds of this new movement could not have been planted in more fertile soil than the northern province of Israel. Through Galilee ran the ancient trade routes between Egypt and Mesopotamia, Syria and Greece. Galilee was literally 'encircled' by Gentiles, a highly populated Jewish enclave hemmed in on three sides by foreigners. The lake, surrounded by steep cliffs and hills, was surrounded by a series of ten crowded lakeside townships, each of some ten thousand inhabitants, a large and turbulent

The calling of Andrew and Peter, by Baroccio. The third man is suggestive of their friend Philip, also a fisherman from Bethsaida.

population concentrated within the deep trench, intense heat and high humidity of the Rift Valley. It was as if the seeds of this new movement had been purposefully planted into a greenhouse atmosphere, where the climatic conditions of the Rift, the Latin temperament of the Galileans, and their frustrated nationalistic hopes combined to make for speedy growth and expansion.

Within this explosive situation, Jesus drew his disciples mainly from the hardy Galilean fishermen. He went to a trade which had no private wrongs and which was content to work from day to day, whose members had both the time and opportunity to escape from the crowds to the peace of the fishing grounds, out on the lake. Thus it is not the jargon of the fanatics, the brigands or the Zealots, but the speech of the fishermen and their simple craft that have become the language and symbolism of Christianity. The Gospels not only reflect the quiet thinking of the fishermen, but the tools and techniques of their trade, their nets, their boats and their catch provided constant illustration for their Master's teaching.

The *beth-saida*(s) were to be found on the northern shores of the lake for a particular reason. The river Jordan flows from the north; fed by the melting snows of Mount Hermon it cascades down the fifty odd miles, descending (that is the literal meaning of its name) some six thousand feet into the lake. The river carries with it a vast load of silt containing a great deal of fish food which attracts shoals from all over the lake.

The best fishing grounds are still to be found near the mouth of the Jordan, at the north-east of the lake. Here on the delta plain, two miles from the river and as far from the lake shore, are the ruins, at El Tell, of a town called Bethsaida (later renamed Julias by Herod Philip, the ruler of Israelite territory east of Jordan and Galilee). The Jewish historian Josephus records that 'he advanced the village of Bethsaida to the dignity of a city, both by the number of inhabitants it contained and also by its other grandeur and called it by the name of Julias, the same name as Caesar's daughter'. The Brothers of Bethsaida, Simon Peter and Andrew, and their friend Philip are as likely to have hailed from Bethsaida Julias as from any other fishing village round the lake. They probably had shacks along the shore where they could dry and mend their nets.

Although the Gospels make no clear reference to a second Bethsaida, nor are there comparable remains on the western shore, nevertheless Mark's Gospel indicates the likelihood of another Bethsaida west of the river. This might well have been a mere fishing suburb of Capernaum and the likely place is at the abundant outflow of hot springs at Tabigha. Here, particularly in the spring, there are excellent catches to be made as fish of all sizes swarm to the warm water loaded with vegetable debris. Here, too, from the early fourth century Christians made pilgrimages to the traditional site of the Feeding of the Five Thousand, in which Andrew played an important part, and to the site of Simon Peter's commission to 'feed my lambs' (John 21).

Matthew's list of the twelve arranges the apostles in pairs, each linked with the word 'and' and beginning with brothers who would naturally go together. This grouping might well not have been a mere editorial arrangement by Matthew, but rather some primitive and functional matching off of brother with brother and friend with friend. It could well be that here was the crew for a twelve-oared boat, with the rowers in pairs side by side on the same thwarts. It is not difficult to imagine Simon Peter and Andrew on the stroke's bench of their boat, with the rest of the crew ranged in pairs behind them, ready to take their rhythm at the oars from the brothers from Bethsaida. Of these two, it was Simon Peter who was the skipper and owner of the fishing smack and Andrew who was the crew-member. Indeed Matthew calls Simon Peter *o protos*, 'the chief', literally 'Number One'. Though so alike in their background and in the skills they had mastered, the inner characters of the two men were widely different, as clearly emerges from the pages of the New Testament.

Simon Peter was the skipper of the crew, but it was his brother Andrew who was the first to be signed on, the *protokletos*, 'the first to be called', as he was named by the early Church. The physical appearance of Peter may have been recorded in an early fourth-century sarcophagus discovered in the Vatican grottoes below St Peter's in Rome. He is of medium height with a large, broad head of curly hair, and a rounded beard. Later representations, such as the sixth-century mosaics in Ravenna, where he is shown in a dinghy with his brother Andrew, became stylized to achieve some sort of contrast between the two great leaders of the Church, Peter and Paul. Peter was depicted with light curly hair, a round beard and a flat nose, while Paul was shown with a bald head, pointed black beard and a large Semitic nose. Early portrayals of Andrew seem to have little in common, but by the sixth century he appears as a tall figure with a long head and a full dark beard.

The character and fortunes of Andrew, the 'first-called' disciple, can be traced through three sources: the Synoptic Gospels, the Fourth Gospel and the mass of apocryphal and legendary material, varying from a third-century apocryphal Acts of Andrew to the fourteenth-century legend of the diagonal cross.

All three Synoptic Gospels – Matthew, Mark and Luke – and the first chapter of the Acts describe the call of Simon Peter and Andrew, though Luke does not mention Andrew by name in his account of the event but adds the story of the miraculous draught of fish and Peter's penitence. 'Passing along by the Sea of Galilee, he saw Simon and Andrew the brother of Simon casting a net in the sea; for they were fishermen.' They must have been in the shallows, casting the small circular nets whose fringe, loaded with lead, drops like a parachute through the water to enclose the fish. 'And Jesus said to them, "Follow me and I will make you become fishers of men." And

Thorwaldsen's portrayal of Andrew follows early tradition: a tall figure with a long head and plentiful dark beard, but includes the diagonal cross of medieval legend.

immediately they left their nets and followed him' (Mark 1 : 16–18).

All three Synoptic Gospels again record that, following the exorcism of an unclean spirit in the synagogue at Capernaum, Jesus entered the home of Peter. Mark adds, 'And immediately he left the synagogue, and entered the house of Simon and Andrew,' implying that the house was directly outside the synagogue and that it was the home of both the brothers as well as of Peter's mother-in-law. An octagonal Byzantine shrine of 'Peter's house' has long been shown opposite the entrance of the site of the synagogue at Capernaum. Recently, however, the Byzantine pavement has been lifted to permit the excavation of first-century houses beneath, thus confirming the occupation of the site in the lifetime of Jesus.

Andrew was present on the Mount of Olives with the inner circle of Jesus's disciples, Peter, James, and John, when Jesus foretold the destruction of the temple and its precincts. The four disciples questioned him privately, 'Tell us, when will this be, and what will be the sign when these things are all to be accomplished?' (Mark 13 : 4). Mark uses their question to introduce the long eschatological discourse about the end of the world which is repeated in both Matthew and Luke.

There is no further reference to Andrew in the first three Gospels, apart from the list of apostles, where he is linked with Philip, as he is also in the list of apostles in the Upper Room before Pentecost.

The Fourth Gospel is far more specific about Andrew and his particular function within the group of disciples. It seems that Andrew and another disciple, possibly Philip, were disciples of John the Baptist during his evangelistic mission by the river Jordan. It was thanks to the word of John the Baptist that these disciples first took notice of Jesus: 'John was standing with two of his disciples; and he looked at Jesus as he walked, and said, "Behold, the Lamb of God!" The two disciples heard him say this, and they followed Jesus. Jesus turned, and saw them following, and said to them, "What do you seek?" And they said to him, "Rabbi" (which means Teacher), "where are you staying?" He said to them, "Come and see." They came and saw where he was staying; and they stayed with him that day' (John 1 : 35–39).

Early next morning Andrew met his brother Simon Peter and declared, 'We have found the Messiah,' and introduced Simon Peter to Jesus. Jesus looked hard at Peter and said, '"So you are Simon the son of John? You shall be called Cephas" (which means Peter).' The writer goes on to mention that Philip, Simon Peter, and Andrew were natives of the same fishing town Bethsaida.

The next reference to Andrew in the Fourth Gospel is in the story of the Feeding of the Five Thousand. His friend Philip, possibly the caterer of the party, has just commented on the fact that two hundred denarii would hardly buy enough bread to give such a crowd even a mouthful apiece. At this point

Galilean Lakeside Townships

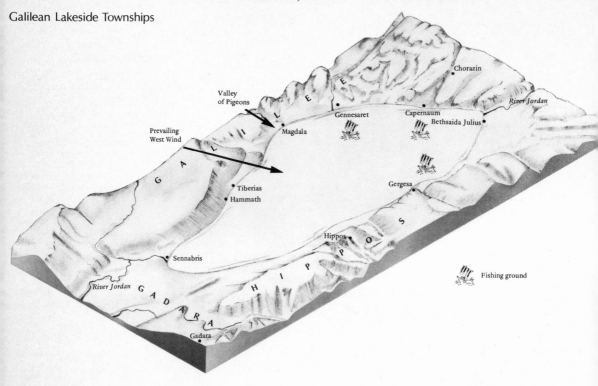

in the dilemma, Andrew produces a little boy with his picnic meal of five barley loaves and two small fishes, saying, 'But what are they among so many?' Nevertheless, he introduces the boy to Jesus, who takes what the boy has to offer, says grace, and divides it for distribution by the disciples. And all are fed.

The last appearance of Andrew is before the Passover festival in Jerusalem, after the triumphal entry on the first Palm Sunday. Some Greeks came up to Philip with the request, 'Sir, we wish to see Jesus.' Philip promptly told his friend Andrew, and together they told Jesus. Andrew once again seems to have been the willing witness and missionary, introducing first his own brother, Peter, then the boy with the loaves and fishes, and finally a Gentile delegation to Jesus.

From this scriptural evidence alone, the character of Andrew emerges with some clarity. Although perhaps physically the larger of the two brothers, he is identified in the lists of Matthew and Luke, as well as in John's narrative of the Feeding of the Five Thousand, as 'the brother of Simon Peter'. Again, although he was the 'first called' and introduced his brother to Jesus, he was rarely included within the 'inner circle'. Compared with his bombastic brother, Andrew emerges as a sensitive and approachable man who always had time and patience to listen to enquiries, even from children and foreigners. He was a selfless and considerate man, who did not resent the leadership of his brother. If his brother, Peter, was the skipper of the crew, Andrew was indeed the 'ferry man' always willing to take people to Jesus. He was a kindly and faithful disciple, not fearful of ridicule even though he offered a picnic basketful to feed five thousand. Although himself a Jew, he enabled Greeks to meet Jesus and he has been called the first 'home mission-ary' as well as the first 'foreign' missionary of the Christian Church.

From the second century a whole series of apocryphal Acts concerning Andrew appear, but most are full of pious fables and contribute little con-firmation of his character as found in the canonical Gospels. The 'Acts of Andrew and Matthias', probably a sixth-century work, describe his activities in 'the town of cannibals', also referred to as 'the town of dogs'. There follow the 'Acts of Peter and Andrew', the 'Acts of Andrew and Bartholomew', the 'Acts of Paul and Andrew'. Such diverse and numerous 'Acts' may preserve the simple historical kernel of fact that Andrew and one other apostle preached the Gospel among a primitive people. There is at least a probability that for part of Andrew's mission, his companion was his brother Peter.

The early tradition of the scattering of the apostles and the allocation of their missionary fields, within the Eleona cave on the Mount of Olives (see p. 9), mentions Scythia as Andrew's region of responsibility. The 'Father of Church History', Eusebius (270–339), confirms this. Now Scythia was the classical term for the wild steppelands beyond the Carpathians and the Caucasus, that is, the territory to the north-east of the Roman Empire, which is today part of south Russia – beyond the Danube and north of the Black Sea. The Scythians were colloquially the uncivilized 'barbarians'; Josephus describes them as 'little different from wild beasts' (Contra Apion 2, 37). Certainly in that area there were no Jewish colonies or synagogues to form a basis for a Christian mission, and the savage populace might figuratively be described as a 'town of cannibals' or 'town of dogs'. Peter's first letter within the New Testament is addressed to 'Pontus, Galatia, Cappadocia, Asia and Bithynia' which, together with Sinope, border on Scythia to the south of the Black Sea. Perhaps it is not surprising that these crude and primitive legends should link the mission of the two brothers, and in the area indicated by Peter's own correspondence, within the New Testament canon.

The second tradition places the sphere of Andrew's mission in Greece. The anonymous second-century 'Acts of Andrew' relate his journey from Pontus, his landing in Achaia, his journey to Macedonia, his sailing to Byzantium, and his return through Thrace and Perinthus to Philippi and Thessalonica where, although thrown to wild beasts in the stadium, Andrew

Rock churches in Cappadocia, carved in the 4th century from cone-shaped mounds, formed by erosion of volcanic lava over an area of 4,000 square miles.

somehow survived. There he had a vision of his brother Peter saying to him, 'Draw near to me, stretch out thy hands so as to join them unto mine, and put thy head by my head. I am the word of the cross whereon thou shalt hang shortly, for his name's sake whom thou preachest.' Andrew warned his disciples of his coming end, gave them his blessing, celebrating the eucharist and commending them to the Lord, then set sail for Patras in

Achaia. Andrew's many journeys provide countless tales of bizarre miracles of healing and exorcism.

On his arrival, he received word that Maximilla, the wife of the newly appointed proconsul, Aegeates, was dying. Andrew went to the governor's house, to find him about to commit suicide as soon as his wife died. Although Andrew healed and converted Maximilla, her husband Aegeates remained strongly opposed to the Christian faith. Stratocles, the brother of Aegeates, had a servant whom Andrew also cured; and Stratocles too became a Christian. Provoked by the conversion of both his wife and his brother, Aegeates the proconsul had Andrew arrested and thrown into prison, where he still continued to preach the Gospel to the other prisoners.

The story of Andrew's martyrdom exists separately in many variant texts, with different versions of his discourses during his suffering. One of these which can be traced to the end of the fourth century was a circular letter, called 'letter of the priests and deacons of Achaia concerning the martyrdom of St Andrew'. This is still used as a lesson in the Roman breviary on St Andrew's Day. The following is a reconstructed text of Andrew's martyrdom.

And he, Andrew, conversed all night with the brethren and prayed with them and committed them to the Lord; afterwards early in the morning the proconsul Aegeates had the prisoner Andrew brought to him and said to him:

'The end of the proceedings against you has come, you stranger, opponent of this present life, and enemy of all my house. For why did you think it good to force your way into places which were no concern of yours and to corrupt a wife who prior to that satisfied me? Why have you done this to me and all Achaia? Therefore receive gifts from me as retaliation for what you have done to me.'

And he gave orders for him to be beaten with seven scourges. After that he ordered he was to be crucified. And he instructed the executioners not to break his legs, intending in that way to make his punishment more severe.

The news now spread abroad throughout all Patrae that the stranger, the righteous man, the slave of Christ, whom Aegeates held prisoner, was being crucified, although he had done nothing wrong; and with one accord they all ran together to the spectacle, angered by the proconsul's impious judgement. When Aegeates's brother, Stratocles, made an abortive attempt to rescue him, Andrew gently chided him.

He said many other things to Stratocles and to those who were going along with them. Then he came to the place where he was to be crucified. And when he saw the cross set in the sand at the sea-shore he left them all and went to the cross and with a strong voice addressed it as if it were a living creature.

One of the most impressive versions of Andrew's prayer of the cross that follows is this:

Hail, precious cross! You have been consecrated by the body of my Lord, and adorned with his limbs as rich jewels. I come to you exulting and glad. Receive me with joy into your arms, O good cross, you have received beauty from our Lord's limbs. I have ardently loved you. Long have I desired and sought you. Now you are found by me, and made ready for my longing soul. Receive me into your arms; take me up from among men, and present me to my Master, that he who redeemed me on you may receive me by you.

Yet another version ends with words to his executioners:

Come hither, ye ministers of joy unto me, ye servants of Aegeates: accomplish the desire of us both, and bind the lamb unto the wood of the offering, the man unto the maker, the soul unto the Saviour.

The Flagellation of Andrew, by Domenichinio, in the Church of St Andrew, Rome, shows his preparation for crucifixion, being 'beaten with seven scourages', at the order of the pro-consul of Achaia.

St Andrew led to his Martyrdom expresses the spirit of his prayer of Approach to the Cross. Painting by Guido Reni in the church of St Gregory, Rome.

The narrative continues:

The blessed Andrew said this standing on the ground and staring steadfastly towards the cross. Then he besought the brethren that the executioners should come and carry out what they had been commanded. For they were standing at a distance.

And they came and bound his hands and his feet and did not nail him; for they had been so instructed by Aegeates. He wished in this way to torture him as he hung in that he would be eaten alive by dogs. And they left him hanging and departed from him.

And when the crowds that stood around who had been made disciples in Christ by him saw that they did none of these things which were usual in the case of crucifixions, they hoped to hear again something from him. For as he hung he moved his head and smiled. And Stratocles asked him: 'Why do you smile, slave of God? Your laughter makes us mourn and weep because we are being deprived of you.' And the blessed Andrew answered him: 'Shall I not laugh, my child Stratocles, at the vain plot of Aegeates by which he intends to avenge himself on us? We are

strangers to him and his designs. He is not capable of hearing. For if he had been capable he would have heard that a man who belongs to Jesus, because he is known to him, is immune from revenge for the future.'

And the crowds who heard his words did not leave the spot; and Andrew continued speaking further to them for a day and a night. And when on the following day they saw his constancy and steadfastness of soul, his wisdom of spirit and strength of mind, they burned with indignation and rushed with one accord to the judgement seat of Aegeates and cried out: 'What, O proconsul, is this judgement of yours? You have condemned wrongly! You have judged unjustly! What wrong has this man done? What transgression has he committed? The whole city is in uproar! You wrong us all! Do not destroy Caesar's city! Hand over to us the righteous man! Give us the holy Man! Do not kill a man who is dear to God! Do not destroy a man [so] gentle and pious! He has hung there for two days and he is still alive. He has eaten nothing but has nourished all of us with his words. And behold, we believe in the God whom he preaches. Take down the righteous man and we will all become philosophers. Set free the ascetic [*lit.* chaste man] and all of Patrae will have peace. Release the wise man and all Achaia will be freed through him.'

Though Aegeates was persuaded by the crowd to visit Andrew, perhaps intending to loose him and take him down, Andrew himself declined saying:

'Let no one release me in any way from these bonds. For there has been allotted me this destiny: to depart out of the body and to live with the Lord, with whom I am even being crucified.'

And the proconsul stood there speechless and as it were out of his mind. When now the whole city noisily demanded that he free Andrew, and he ventured to approach the cross to unloose him and take him down, Andrew cried out loudly: 'Do not permit, Lord, that Andrew who has been bound up to thy cross, should be set free. Do not give me up, who am on thy mystery [Narr.: hang on thy mystery], to the shameless devil. O Jesus Christ, let not thy adversary loose me who hang on thy grace. Father, let this little one no longer humiliate him who has known thy greatness, Jesus Christ, whom I have seen, whom I have, whom I love, in whom I am and will be, receive me in peace into thy eternal tabernacles, that through my exodus the many who are akin [in nature] to me may enter to thee and may rest in thy majesty.'

And after the death of the blessed Andrew, Maximilla came with Stratocles without a thought of those who were standing around and took down the body of Andrew. And when the evening came she buried him.

In 337 his coffin was transferred at the command of the Emperor Constantine to Byzantium, later known as Constantinople and today as Istanbul. A legend still current in Amalfi, in the Bay of Salerno, records that following the capture of Byzantium by the Fourth Crusade in 1204 a certain Cardinal Capuana 'took secretly' the relics of St Andrew and enshrined them at Amalfi. There they were visited by St Francis of Assisi and St Bridget of

The Death of St Andrew, by Mattia Preti, in St Andrew's Church, Rome, follows the 14th-century tradition of the diagonal cross, suggested perhaps by apocryphal record that he was bound, not nailed.

Ruins of the magnificent church of Regulus, who landed on the coast of Fife with relics of Andrew and became first bishop of the ancient Scottish town of St Andrew's.

Sweden. Since 1304, on the vigil of St Andrew (29 November) the skull has been reported to exude a kind of 'manna', much treasured by the Amalfitans.

Only recently, Pope John XXIII gave a reliquary – said to contain face bones of St Andrew – to the Greek Orthodox Church.

The final strand of legend links Andrew with Scotland. In the seventh century a certain monk called Regulus, so the story runs, pillaged a parcel of bones from the relics of St Andrew in Constantinople. Regulus travelled westwards until he landed on the coast of Fife, where he convinced

St Peter's, Rome, the mother church of Catholic Christendom, whose grandeur reflects the devotion accorded to Peter as Prince and Shepherd of the Church.

Nechtan, a newly converted king of the Picts, that these bones were authentic relics of the apostle. Regulus became the first bishop of St Andrews, and the ruins of his magnificent church are still to be seen in the most ancient university town of Scotland.

The Picts and the English in those days were at war. The night before the decisive battle, Andrew is said to have appeared in advance to Hungus, another king of the Picts, to promise him victory. On the following day, writes William Barclay of Glasgow, 'a shining cross was seen in the sky straight above the army of the Picts, not unlike the same cross that the apostle died on. This cross vanished never out of the sky till the victory succeeded to the Picts. The Picts advanced to the battle with the cry, "St Andrew, our patron, be our guide!" They utterly defeated the English who had been terrified seeing the cross shine with awful beams in the sky.'

Since about 750, Andrew has been the patron saint of the Scots and his white cross on a sky-blue background has been their standard. Not until the fourteenth century, however, did the tradition of the 'X'-shaped cross appear, presumably because the 'X' was the Greek 'Ch', and the first letter of the Greek word *'Christos'*, or Messiah.

About the same time, the remaining relics of Andrew were transferred to Rome, where reputedly they lie below the great cathedral of his brother

Roman statue in St Peter's. The head was replaced by one of Peter in the 13th century, and the hands by ones holding keys in the 14th century.

Peter. There, in the central crossing, facing the gospel or north side of the high altar, standing within a niche of one of the four huge piers that support the famous dome of Michelangelo, is a fifteen-foot statue of Andrew. Across the nave and beside a similar statue of Longinus, the centurion at the Crucifixion, is the famous statue of Peter, a bronze figure in a marble chair. These two statues are a reminder of the paramount importance of the two brothers from Bethsaida to the growth and mission of the Church in the world. The brothers of Bethsaida, who bent their oars on the same bench of their boat on Galilee, came in old age to a similar supreme sacrifice through crucifixion. The one died of exposure on a sea shore, not nailed but roped to his cross. The other died probably of asphyxiation in a Roman circus, cruci-fied upside down.

The scale of St Peter's, for half the Christians in the world regarded as the mother church of Christendom, testifies to the respect and devotion accorded to Peter and also to his brother Andrew. Catholic Christendom has always regarded Peter, the first shepherd of the Church, as the first in an unbroken line of pontiffs, commanding near and far, '*urbi et orbi*', the city and the world. The claims of successive 'bishops of Rome' to inherit the place of Peter and to occupy the chair of Peter within the universal Church have been based upon an appropriation of Jesus's charge to Peter, following Peter's confession that Jesus was Messiah. 'And I tell you, you are Peter, and on this rock I will build my church, and the powers of death shall not prevail against it. I will give you the keys of the kingdom of heaven, and whatever you bind on earth shall be bound in heaven, and whatever you loose on earth shall be loosed in heaven' (Matt. 16:18–19). Acceptance of such claims for the Papacy still depend upon the interpretation of 'apostleship' and 'apostolic succession'. No Christians however would be likely to dispute the Apostle Peter's authority in the Kingdom of Heaven. For all Christians he is the eternal doorkeeper and the eternal bearer of the keys, 'no gaoler but the guard of eternal freedom'.

Of all the personalities in the New Testament, perhaps we know most about the character of Peter. He is the most attractive for his constant mis-takes and subsequent forgiveness, his boisterous and impetuous enthusiasm, and for his good intentions and self-confidence that so soon seemed to dis-appear. At first he seems to have been a surprising choice as the 'Rock' upon which Jesus was to found his Church, but he justified his choice by an example that has inspired and encouraged Christians down the centuries.

He became one of the closest friends of Jesus and the natural leader of 'the twelve', and although his leadership seems to have been superseded by Paul, Peter became the traditional first bishop of Rome. His tomb is reputed to have been excavated below the high altar of the great Roman basilica of St Peter's.

The scriptural sources of information about Peter include all four

The Catacombs of St Sebastian, under the Via Appia, where traditionally the relics of Peter rested before entombment beneath the 4th-century Constantinian Basilica of St Peter's.

Gospels, Acts, Galatians, 1 Corinthians, as well as the correspondence attributed to Peter himself. The most important, however, is the Gospel of Mark. For the link between Peter and this Gospel there is both external and internal evidence.

The external is to be found in the tradition of the early Church. The earliest known reference to Mark's Gospel is to be found in Eusebius, who reported Papias, bishop of Hierapolis, as saying in a document which has since been lost: 'This also the Elder said: "Mark, having become the interpreter of Peter, wrote down accurately all that he remembered of the things done and said by Christ, but not however in order. For neither did he

[Mark] hear the Lord speak, nor did he follow him, but afterwards, as I have said, he followed Peter."' If the elder referred to is the writer of the second and third epistles of John, the statement may be traced to the writer of the fourth Gospel – who himself made use of Mark's original Gospel.

Irenaeus (*c.* 185) writes: 'And after their deaths [referring to Peter and Paul], Mark, the disciple and interpreter of Peter, himself also handed down to us in writing the things which Peter had proclaimed.' Tradition dates the deaths of the two leaders of the Church as approximately AD 64, during the persecution of Christians by Nero. Clement of Alexandria (*c.* 200) says that Mark wrote at Rome during the lifetime of Peter; and Tertullian of Africa and Origen of Asia (both *c.* 225) agree that Mark recorded in writing the reminiscences of Peter.

The internal evidence is equally convincing. The traditional association of Mark with Peter has been amply proven by study of the Gospel itself. The Gospel in outline resembles closely Peter's speech to Cornelius at Caesarea.

The Last Prayer, a 19th-century engraving by Gérome, evokes the excitement and tragedy of a spectacle in the Circus Maximus or Colosseum.

Bust of the Emperor Nero, in the Museum Delle Terme, Naples. During his persecution, both St Peter and St Paul, the prince-apostles, met their martyrdoms c. 64.

Its vivid reality, detail, frankness (and minor inaccuracies) reflect the character of Peter. From the final greetings of Peter's first letter, we might infer that 'Mark, my son', as Peter calls him, was at Rome assisting Peter. Most scholars interpret 'Babylon' as an apocalyptic reference to Rome; but a few consider that it refers to Bablun, the Roman fortress in Old Cairo, and are quick to point out Mark's association with Egypt. The emphasis within Mark's Gospel upon suffering, and upon the inevitability of the individual taking up his cross, indicates that the Gospel was written for a martyr church – during persecution probably in Rome. What could have been more appropriate than that the first and original Gospel should be written at the very hub of the civilized world and that the Gospel should record the reminiscences and teaching of the earliest leader and spokesman of the apostles? Who could have been better qualified than Mark, the missionary companion of Paul and the secretary of Peter, to write a biography of Jesus upon which successive Gospels have been based?

Simon Peter is called by no less than four different names within the New Testament besides his patronymic. Each of these, and especially the patronymic, has a particular significance. Simon was the Greek form of the Hebrew name Simeon, by which he was known in strict Jewish circles, as by James the brother of Jesus (Acts 15:14) and in the Judaeo–Christian Church at Jerusalem (2 Pet. 1:1). He was the son of a certain John, or more probably *Jonah*, which name means 'a dove'. When Peter was introduced to Jesus, he greeted him and said, 'You shall be called Cephas', the Aramaic word for *rock*, of which the Greek translation is *Petros* (John 1:42). The disciples seem to have used the Greek form *Petros* or Peter, though Paul called him '*Cephas*' in his first letter to Corinth and that to Galatia, apparently preferring the Aramaic form.

'Simon, son of John' may just be an allusion to his previous discipleship of John the Baptist, but it is possible to interpret Jesus's greeting as: 'So you are Simon, son of the Dove, you shall be the Rock.' The term 'son of' so often implies 'with the character of' that the contrast between the shy little Palestinian dove and the rugged stability of a rock would have been very obvious. Those who heard, among them Andrew and perhaps the sons of Zebedee, could not have failed to be amused at their broad-shouldered friend with the name of 'the dove' being renamed 'the rock'!

In the Gospels, Peter's character appears to be at variance with the nickname of the 'Rock', given to him by Jesus. Whether his name was to describe his physique or his temperament, that name was prophetically confirmed by Jesus at Caesarea Philippi and amply justified by his granite-like leadership of the apostles from Pentecost onwards. He was always a man of action, but from his calling by Jesus to his denial of Jesus he was a man of impulse and aggressive energy, of childlike simplicity and daring, alternating with a weak and cowardly instability.

The turning-points in Peter's life were the appearance of Jesus to him after the Resurrection, and Jesus's threefold question and commission to him to 'feed my sheep'. Certainly from Pentecost onwards he was the true and undoubted leader of the Church, facing without fear the consequent persecution and punishment, and doing so with an inspiring courage and humility. This humility is strikingly illustrated in the Gospel of Mark, which shows him in a far less favourable light than do the other three Gospels! This is particularly striking when it is remembered that Mark's Gospel has been said by Irenaeus, as early as the year 185, to have been based on the reminiscences of Peter, the 'mind behind' the Second Gospel.

The Miraculous Catch (in broad daylight following a fruitless night's fishing), reflects the admiration and amazement of the brothers. Painting by G. de Dreyer.

It was soon after Peter's introduction to Jesus that Jesus prevailed over the fisherman's greater experience and persuaded him to shoot his nets in daylight after a fruitless night's fishing. The two pairs of brothers, James and John, Peter and Andrew, were completely overcome by the remarkable catch which they then made, and they were called by Jesus to follow him in full-time training to become 'fishers of men' (Mark 1:16–20).

From then onwards, Peter's house at Capernaum became the head-quarters of Jesus's lakeside ministry, and Peter's boat was always at his disposal. The selection of the team of twelve disciples was completed, and Peter was always included at the head of the list. Perhaps this was not so much because he was acknowledged as leader by the other disciples, as the result of the fact that his household was the headquarters of the group and that he and Andrew were its first members.

With James and John, Peter formed an inner circle of three, who alone were allowed to accompany Jesus into the house for the raising of Jairus's daughter, to witness the Transfiguration, and to share the agony in the Garden of Gethsemane. Peter was often the spokesman of the twelve, and was their natural leader. He walked on the water. He spoke loyally for

The reconstructed synagogue at Capernaum. Within yards of the entrance towards the lakeside, beneath an octagonal Byzantine mosaic, have been excavated the remains of 1st-century houses.

the others when Jesus's teaching about the 'bread of life' (John 6:66–69) scandalized them. He expressed the conviction of the twelve when he made his great confession at Caesarea Philippi: 'You are the Christ, the Son of the living God.' At once Jesus replied, 'You are Peter, and on this rock I will build my Church, and the powers of death shall not prevail against it. I will give you the keys of the kingdom of heaven . . .' (Matt. 16:18–19). Peter's confession of faith, however, was followed by a sharp rebuke, because he refused to listen to Jesus's first prediction of his Passion. In his capacity as leader, Peter was approached by the tax-collectors for the temple tribute due from Jesus and his disciples. He was constantly voicing the questions of the twelve about the limits of forgiveness, and about the destruction of the temple.

Peter's role in the Passion story was considerable. Together with John, he was entrusted with the preparations for the Last Supper, in which Jesus clearly confirmed his leadership 'when you have turned again' (Luke 22:32), and at once foretold the threefold denial, which Peter passionately contradicted; Peter also protested at the feet-washing, and then impetuously demanded that Jesus wash him completely. Peter beckoned John to ask

Peter's fishing smack and his walking on the water, possibly by Taddio Gaddi, in the Church of St Maria Novella, Florence.

The Kiss of Judas, by Barna da Siena. In the foreground Peter strikes a blow in defence
of Jesus, cutting the ear of the high priest's servant, Malchus.

ABOVE Christ washing Peter's feet, by Ford Maddox Brown, emphasises the simplicity and humility in Jesus's example of menial domestic service.

Jesus the identity of the betrayer; and although chosen to keep watch with James and John in the Garden of Gethsemane, Peter slept with them. At the moment of arrest, however, it was Peter who struck out in defence of Jesus with his sword – only to be rebuked by Jesus. When all the rest fled, Peter followed at a distance to the high priest's palace, where he was admitted to the court after the intervention of John with the portress. There he was accused of being one of Jesus's followers, denied three times that he knew Jesus, then remembered Jesus's prediction and repented bitterly. Luke adds that 'the Lord turned and looked at Peter' (Luke 22:61). If Mark's account of the trial before the Sanhedrin may be said to reveal the lack of witnesses of Jesus's admission to being the Christ, for which he was condemned as a blasphemer, then perhaps Peter's denial might well have prevented Peter himself being forced to give evidence of Jesus's Messiahship.

Peter may well have spoken colloquial Greek, but his native language

OPPOSITE Peter's denial in the High Priest's Palace, and his subsequent penitence at cock-crow, may conceal his refusal to reveal his identity as a potential prosecution witness. Painted by Carl Bloch.

The Crucifixion of St Peter, by Michaelangelo,
from the Chapel of St Paul, in the Vatican.
Eusebius and Origen confirm that he was
crucified upside-down, during Nero's reign.

would have been Aramaic; thus his Galilean brogue would have been all too obvious to the bystanders at the trial. 'And as Peter was below in the courtyard, one of the maids of the high priest came; and seeing Peter warming himself, she looked at him and said, "You also were with the Nazarene, Jesus." But he denied it, saying, "I neither know nor understand what you mean." And he went out into the gateway. And the maid saw him, and began again to say to the bystanders, "This man is one of them." But again he denied it. And after a little while again the bystanders said to Peter, "Certainly you are one of them; for you are a Galilean."' (Mark 14:66–70).

Various churches have been built on the possible sites of the high priest's palace to commemorate the trial and imprisonment of Jesus by Caiaphas, as well as Peter's denial and repentance. Some place the site on the top of the Western Hill, near the Armenian chapel, others prefer the remains covered by the Church of St Peter *in Gallicantu*, 'of the cock-crowing'. Here the story can be vividly reconstructed. Within the present church, over the high altar, is an illustration of the trial, which was conducted in the rock-hewn courtyard on the next level below the church. The prisoner is standing on a raised platform, chained by the wrists to escorts seated on either side of him. It is easy to picture this scene on the lower level, facing westwards into the hillside in which are cut staircases and galleries. On one of these Peter must have sat with the soldiers, warmed himself by the fire, and denied knowing his master. On either side of the wall, behind the raised dock platform, the corners of the courtyard are cut square to a height of ten feet. In the very centre of the courtroom is the mouth of a bottle-necked prison, into which the condemned prisoner could be lowered after trial. Descending to a third level, there is a complete guardroom, all round the walls of which are still to be found the staples for the prisoners' chains (some consider this to have been a stable in Byzantine times). On one side there is a small window opening on to the bottle-necked condemned cell. Below this window, and left projecting from the floor when the guardroom was excavated from the living rock, is a block on which the guard stood to peer down into the gloom of the cell below him.

On the opposite side of the guardroom is the whipping-block. Here, tied up by the wrists with leather thongs through staples at the top, a belt round his waist secured to a staple at each side, the prisoner would be stretched up, taut and helpless. At his feet were two bowls, carved in the rock, one for salt to disinfect his wounds, one for vinegar to revive him. Here, both Peter and John received the legal sentence of 'forty lashes less one', thirteen on each shoulder from the back, and thirteen on the chest from the front, were commanded not to preach Jesus as Christ, and then sent home. Yet they returned daily to the temple to preach this very thing.

The Gospels do not mention Peter from the night of Jesus's trial to the morning of his Resurrection, but the writer of the first letter of Peter says that he was 'a witness of the sufferings of Christ' (5 : 1). On Easter morning, Peter and John ran to the tomb, to find it empty. Both Luke and Paul report that Jesus appeared to Peter alone on the day of the Resurrection. Certainly he shared with several others the appearance by the Lake of Galilee. Then John recognized Jesus; but Peter swam ashore to share the breakfast cooked on the fire of coals. There, Peter's love was three times tested for his three-fold denial: 'Simon, son of John, do you love me?' (John 21). Peter then received his threefold commission to shepherd the flock of God. There, too, he received the prediction of his martyrdom. And there today the remains of the medieval chapel of 'Peter's Primacy' enclose a vast rock which projects out into the clear waters of the lake. The rock, known as the 'Table of the Lord', is still in its striking simplicity a silent witness to the Resurrection tradition in Galilee and to the commission of Peter as 'prince of the apostles'.

After Jesus's Ascension, at which he 'sent out' his apostles into the world, Peter at once assumed the leadership of the apostles. He suggested the choice of a replacement for Judas. He spoke for the apostles on the day of Pentecost, with great inspiration and effect. He was the first of the apostles to perform a miracle in the name of Jesus – healing the cripple at the Beautiful Gate of the Temple. He conducted the defence of John and himself before the Sanhedrin, and pronounced the condemnation of Ananias and Sapphira. He was soon renowned for his miracles done in the name of Jesus, and he and John were sent to Samaria where, through the laying-on of their hands, the Holy Spirit came to the baptized believers.

It was Peter who healed Aeneas, the paralytic, at Lydda, and who raised to life Dorcas, the woman of Joppa renowned for her good works. While in Joppa (now Jaffa), Peter received a vision convincing him, as he admitted, that 'God shows no partiality, but in every nation any one who fears him and does what is right is acceptable to him'. He then converted and baptized Cornelius, a Roman centurion, and his whole household at Caesarea (Acts 10). At the Council of Jerusalem he upheld his decision to do this and was supported by Paul and Barnabas.

We know little of Peter's work outside Palestine. Paul mentions Peter's visit to Antioch (Gal. 2 : 11–21), where he yielded to the demands of certain Jewish-Christians in dissociating himself temporarily from the Gentiles. Peter seems to have visited Corinth (1 Cor. 1 : 12), and he may well have been engaged in evangelism in Rome itself before Paul's arrival (Rom. 15 : 20–22). Certainly, Eusebius and Origen declare that he went to Rome and, as an old man, suffered martyrdom by crucifixion head downwards, during the reign of Nero, probably in AD 64.

The site of the present St Peter's Church in Rome, and of the first Constantinian basilica there, has been venerated by Christians from the earliest times as the site of the tomb of Peter. The first memorial over his

The miraculous Deliverance of Peter by the Angel, from his prison in Jerusalem, when arrested at the order of Herod Agrippa.

grave was built in about 160. A vast five-aisled basilica was built by Constantine on the Vatican Hill above the traditional site of the grave. Two series of excavations instituted by Pope Paul XII, from 1940–51 and from 1953–7, have established what if anything has survived of the original grave. The apostle's body was certainly buried on the Vatican Hill, at a spot close to the gardens of Nero and their famous circus or sports stadium. The grave would have been a plain earth trench covered with large tiles. In time this whole area came to be one of the largest burial grounds in Rome, and the apostle's grave would have become hemmed in by others, dating back to about the year 70 or 80. There are second- or early third-century Greek *graffiti*, cut in a dividing wall above the traditional site of the grave, which refer to Peter.

Of the two letters ascribed to Peter, the first is more likely to reflect the teaching and message of Peter himself than the second, which was written and attributed to him at least a hundred years after his death. The first is a message to the Churches in northern Asia Minor to help them meet the shock of sudden and violent persecution, to strengthen and reassure them in the faith, and to encourage them to remain firm in their allegiance to God. After the greeting there follows a long, perhaps baptismal discourse, unlike a simple letter in form or content, and without any personal or local references. This may have been a separate composition, with its own introduction and conclusion in the form of a sermon on the nature of the Christian life.

The letter assumes a basic knowledge of the Christian faith and it instructs the readers accordingly about baptism, regeneration, the nature of God, the sufferings of Jesus, and the Christian hope. The references to suffering and trials are of a general nature and do not indicate existing persecution. The mere profession of Christianity does not incur punishment, indeed those innocent of any wrongdoing can expect to be vindicated by the Roman magistrate. The Greek is excellent, the tone calm and tranquil.

The letter then begins to reflect an atmosphere of tension. The style is simple and direct, the language quick and nervous. Suffering is now a stark reality and their faith is put to the test; they are being persecuted for the very name of Christian by the authorities. Now is their judgement, their opportunity to share the sufferings of Christ in the brotherhood of his Church, that they may share his glory. The letter closes with greetings and the bearer was Silvanus.

There is a disagreement among scholars about the authorship of this letter. Some accept that it was written by Peter, explaining its style and language as the work of Silvanus, the secretary. In that case the persecution referred to must be Nero's of AD 64. But that persecution did not extend to the provinces of Asia Minor and Christianity did not reach Pontus by the Black Sea before AD 65. There was persecution of Christians under the Emperor Trajan (98–117) in Bithynia and Pontus, where the governor was

Pliny the Younger. Pliny's own records of examinations under torture both of men and women have survived and accord with the description in I Peter. The letter is first described by Polycarp in AD 135, so must have been written between AD 65 and 135. It may perhaps be the composite work of Peter, Silvanus and another writer, adapting it to the needs of a later persecution, using the name of Peter as a suitable martyr-apostle to encourage the suffering Christians of his time. The letter is important as not teaching the doctrine of a single author, but as a systematic presentation of the faith of the early Christian Church.

The so-called second epistle of Peter was undoubtedly written in the second century under the name of Peter, in order to discredit views which the author thought unapostolic. The Greek style and the general tone was absolutely different from I Peter. Eusebius, writing in the fourth century, roundly declares that of all the writings in the name of Peter, 'only one epistle is genuine'. Certainly, this letter, 2 Peter, is dependent upon that of Jude. References to all Paul's letters also show that it was not written until after they had been collected into one corpus. The letter denounces false teachers with all the authority of an apostle. The inclusion within the New Testament of this letter is not based upon its authorship, but upon its intrinsic value recognized by the Church as the authentic voice of apostolic teaching.

With the exception of Peter's discourses in the Acts of the Apostles, and perhaps of the two Petrine epistles, the writings attributed to Peter are apocryphal and unreliable. Nevertheless, because such legendary material often bears a kernel of truth, it is well worth examination. By way of contrast, however, let us look at Peter's remarkable sermon to Cornelius the centurion at Caesarea.

You know the word which he sent to Israel, preaching good news of peace by Jesus Christ (he is Lord of all), the word which was proclaimed throughout all Judaea, beginning from Galilee after the baptism which John preached: how God anointed Jesus of Nazareth with the Holy Spirit and with power; how he went about doing good and healing all that were oppressed by the devil, for God was with him. And we are witnesses to all that he did both in the country of the Jews and in Jerusalem. They put him to death by hanging him on a tree; but God raised him on the third day and made him manifest; not to all the people but to us who were chosen by God as witnesses, who ate and drank with him after he rose from the dead. And he commanded us to preach to the people, and to testify that he is the one ordained by God to be judge of the living and the dead. To him all the prophets bear witness that every one who believes in him receives forgiveness of sins through his name (Acts 10:36–43).

Not only was this occasion a unique event in the extension of the Church to the non-Jewish world, but it represents a superb summary of the

Christian Gospel, expressed with all the simplicity, sincerity and directness of an eyewitness to the actual events. The apocryphal works are clearly retrospective and often polemical – that is, designed to 'grind an axe' for some contemporary doctrinal purpose – though with the best intentions and with great devotion and admiration for the 'Prince of the Apostles'.

There appear to have been five distinct sources or documents concerning Peter which did not find inclusion within the New Testament canon. They have come down in so many versions and translations that it is difficult to put them in any definite chronological order of appearance. The 'Proclamation of Peter', probably Egyptian in origin, was in circulation during the first half of the second century, though the work has been almost completely lost but for a few surviving fragments. It was known and accepted in its entirety by Clement of Alexandria in the second half of that century and to Origen in the first half of the third century, but that great Alexandrian biblical critic did not regard it as genuine.

The 'Proclamation of Peter' was largely a summary of Christian mission-ary propaganda, exalting Christian monotheism in contrast to the current beliefs of Jews and Greeks. This passage, quoted by Clement, expresses the purpose of the work:

I have chosen you twelve because I judged you worthy to be my disciples (whom the Lord wishes). And I sent them, of whom I was persuaded that they would be true apostles, into the world to proclaim to men in all the world the joyous message that they may know that there is [only] one God, and to reveal what future happen-ings there would be through belief on me [Christ], to the end that those who hear and believe may be saved; and that those who believe not may testify that they have heard it and not be able to excuse themselves saying, 'We have not heard' (Strom. vi.6.48).

The 'Apocalypse of Peter', also belonging to the first half of the second century and also known to Clement of Alexandria, was classified as spurious by both Eusebius and by the great biblical scholar Jerome (c. 342–420). This was as well known as the 'Revelation of John' and was read in the Palestinian Good Friday liturgy until the fifth century. The writer depicted the beauties of heaven and the horrors of hell. In heaven the departed lived in a world of beauty, brightness and sunlight, the air perfumed with spice and fruit. It was a place of praise and harmony. Hell, in contrast, was a place of perpetual pain and torment, of fire, filth and unending frustration, where the punishment was made to fit the crime.

And opposite these were still other men and women who bit through their tongues and had flaming fire in their mouths. These were the false witnesses. And in another place were glowing pebbles, sharper than any sword or any spit, and men and women, clad in filthy rags, rolled upon them in torment. These were they who were rich and trusted in their riches and had no mercy upon orphans and widows, but despised the commandment of God. And in another great lake, full of discharge and blood and boiling mire, stood men and women up to their knees. They were those who lent money and demanded compound interest. And I saw the murderers and their accessories cast into a gorge full of venomous reptiles and tormented by those beasts, and thus writhing in that torture, and worms oppressed them like dark clouds. But the souls of those who had been murdered stood and watched the punishment of those murderers and said 'O God, righteous is thy judgement'.

The 'Gospel of Peter', of the same period and possibly of Syrian origin, was used by the early Christian apologist Justin Martyr (*c.* 100–165) and was certainly known to Serapion, bishop of Antioch in 190, as well as to Origen. Only a fragment of this largely legendary work has survived. Its author cast doubt on the reality of the sufferings of Jesus and upon the reality of his human body. He was also extremely anti-Jewish, putting all the blame for the Passion of Jesus entirely on the Jews and 'whitewashing' Pilate.

The 'Acts of Peter', circulated during the second half of the second century and about the same length as Mark's Gospel, was probably written in Asia. The 'Acts' was translated into several languages and versions of various fragments of it have survived. The Latin version, *Actus Vercellenses*, still to be found *in toto*, relates the conflict of Peter and Simon Magus, the magician. There are stories of fantastic contests of power between the two Simons. A dog and baby were used as messengers by Peter to Simon, the dog barking and the baby crying. Simon caused a dead man's head to move, but Peter raised him to life. Simon Magus is mentioned only briefly in the Acts of the Apostles, chapter 8, but he must have been a powerful magician, whose followers – the Simonians – were still a strong sect in the second century. There are two conflicting tales of Simon's downfall. A third-century writer, Hippolytus, states that Simon asked to be buried alive in order to demonstrate his power to survive, but that he failed to rise. The 'Acts of Peter' relates his dramatic downfall while attempting to fly over the Roman forum.

And by the following day a large crowd had assembled on the Sacred Way to see him fly. And Peter, having seen a vision, came to the place, in order to convict him again this time; for when [Simon] made his entry into Rome, he astonished the crowds by flying; but Peter, who exposed him, was not yet staying in Rome, [the city] which he so carried away by his deceptions that people lost their senses through him. So this man stood on a high place, and seeing Peter, he began to say: 'Peter, now of all times, when I am making my ascent before all these onlookers, I tell you: If your god has power enough – he whom the Jews destroyed, and they stoned you who were chosen by him – let him show that faith in him is of God; let it be shown at this time whether it be worthy of God. For I by ascending will show to all this crowd what manner of being I am.' And lo and behold, he was carried up into the air, and

everyone saw him all over Rome, passing over its temples and its hills; while the faithful looked towards Peter. And Peter, seeing the incredible sight, cried out to the Lord Jesus Christ, 'Let this man do what he undertook, and the signs and wonders which thou gavest them through me shall be disbelieved. Make haste, Lord, with thy grace, and let him fall down from [this] height, and be crippled, but not die; but let him be disabled and break his leg in three places!' And he fell down from that height and broke his leg in three places. Then they stoned him and went to their own homes; but from that time they all believed in Peter.

A Coptic version includes Peter's miraculous healing of his paralysed daughter for the conviction of his friends and then her return to her sickbed. The Greek version tells the '*Domine quo vadis*' legend and describes the crucifixion of Peter. It is possible that the 'Martyrdom' section of the Acts may be rather later than the rest.

Yet another document, a 'History of Peter and Paul', was circulated in the third century to prove the personal unity of these two great apostles and to combat heretical theories about a conflict of doctrine. This document claims to describe the martyrdom of Paul.

The *Ecclesiastical History* of Eusebius at various points confirms and

comments upon the apocryphal material mentioned, but particularly upon the 'Acts of Peter'. He refers to Simon the Magician as being convicted by Peter in Samaria of his wickedness, and to Simon's flight to Rome, where he continued his sorceries. Eusebius adds that Peter, 'that powerful and great apostle, who by his courage took lead of all the rest', dealt with that 'pest of all mankind'.

Eusebius remarks that Peter 'appears to have preached through Pontus, Galatia, Bithynia, Cappadocia and Asia, who also finally coming to Rome, was crucified head downwards, at his own request'. 'They say,' says the historian, 'that Peter wrote in Rome itself, as is indicated by him, when, by a figure he calls the city Babylon.' It is Eusebius who relates that Peter's wife was crucified before Peter himself and that Peter, compelled to watch, encouraged her with the words 'Remember the Lord'. Peter's behaviour led even his gaoler to become a Christian. Elsewhere he comments, 'Paul is said to have been beheaded at Rome and Peter to have been crucified. . . . This account is confirmed by the fact that the names of Peter and Paul still remain in the cemeteries of that city even to this day.' Another ecclesiastical historian, Caius, born at the turn of the second century, writes 'I can show you the graves of the apostles: for if you will go to the Vatican, or to the Ostian road, you will find the graves of those who have laid the foundations of the Church, and that both suffered martyrdom about the same time.'

The events which led up to the martyrdom of Peter are described at length in the 'Acts of Peter'. These events took place at the very centre of Christendom in Rome, and within about eighty-five years this record was in circulation. Those who would have read it would have been second-generation Christians, whose parents would remember the places and the personalities concerned. The actual sequence of events, and particularly the statements of Peter and his persecutors, will inevitably have been coloured by the interpretation and purpose of the author. But, even in this twentieth century, we cannot agree about the facts or fallacies of the sinking of the *Titanic* or *Lusitania* only sixty years ago. Nevertheless, this narrative must enshrine a thread of truth linking the events described, and similarly the spirit of the apostle breaks through the verbose and sugary piety of the author's presentation.

Peter's preaching, probably on the threefold call to poverty, chastity and obedience, began to take effect on the lives and families of public men in Rome, particularly the prefect Agrippa and a friend of Caesar called Albinus.

But Peter stayed in Rome and rejoiced with the brethren in the Lord and gave thanks night and day for the mass of people who were daily added to the holy name by the grace of the Lord. And the concubines of the prefect Agrippa also came to Peter, being four in number, Agrippina and Nicaria and Euphemia and Doris. And hearing the preaching of purity and all the words of the Lord they were cut to the heart and agreed with each other to remain in purity [renouncing] intercourse with

Agrippa; and they were molested by him.

Now when Agrippa was perplexed and distressed about them – for he loved them passionately – he made inquiries, and when he sent [to find out] where they had gone, he discovered that [they had gone] to Peter. And when they came [back] he said to them, 'That Christian has taught you not to consort with me; I tell you, I will both destroy you and burn him alive.' They therefore took courage to suffer every injury from Agrippa, [wishing] only to be vexed by passion no longer, being strengthened by the power of Jesus.

But one woman who was especially beautiful, the wife of Albinus the friend of Caesar, Xanthippe by name, came with the other ladies to Peter, and she too separated from Albinus. He therefore, filled with fury, and passionate love for Xanthippe, and amazed that she would not even sleep in the same bed with him, was raging like a wild beast and wished to do away with Peter; for he knew he was responsible for her leaving his bed. And many other women besides fell in love with the doctrine of purity and separated from their husbands, and men too ceased to sleep with their own wives, since they wished to worship God in sobriety and purity.

So there was great disquiet in Rome; and Albinus put his case to Agrippa, and said to him, 'Either you must get me satisfaction from Peter, who caused my wife's separation, or I shall do it myself'; and Agrippa said that he had been treated in the same way by him, by the separation of his concubines. And Albinus said to him, 'Why then do you delay, Agrippa? Let us find him and execute him as a trouble-maker, so that we may recover our wives, and in order to give satisfaction to those who cannot execute him, who have themselves been deprived of their wives by him.'

Peter was warned by his friends to escape from Rome and left the city, only to be met by a vision of Jesus entering the city to be crucified in his stead. Peter then recovered himself and returned to await his arrest.

But while they made these plans Xanthippe discovered her husband's conspiracy with Agrippa and sent and told Peter, so that he might withdraw from Rome. And the rest of the brethren together with Marcellus entreated him to withdraw. But Peter said to them, 'Shall we act as deserters, brethren?' But they said to him, 'No, it is so that you can go on serving the Lord.' So he assented to the brethren and withdrew by himself, saying, 'Let none of you retire with me, but I shall retire by myself in disguise.' And as he went out of the gate he saw the Lord entering Rome: and when he saw him he said, 'Lord, whither [goest thou] here?' And the Lord said to him, 'I am coming to Rome to be crucified.' And Peter said to him, 'Lord, art thou being crucified again?' He said to him, 'Yes, Peter, I am being crucified again.' And Peter came to himself; and he saw the Lord ascending into heaven; then he returned to Rome rejoicing and giving praise to the Lord.

So he returned to the brethren and told them what had been seen by him; and they were grieved at heart, and said with tears, 'We entreat you, Peter, take thought for us that are young.' And Peter said to them, 'If it is the Lord's will, it is coming to pass even if we will not have it so. But the Lord is able to establish you in your faith in him, and he will lay your foundation on him and enlarge you in him, [you] whom he himself has planted, so that you may plant others through him. But

79

The Stoning of Stephen, by Angelico, from the Vatican; an event which precipitated the early dispersion of Hellenized Christians throughout the Mediterranean world.

as for me, so long as the Lord wills me to be in the flesh, I do not demur; again, if he will take me, I rejoice and am glad.'

And while Peter was saying this and all the brethren were in tears, four soldiers arrested him and took him to Agrippa. And he in his distemper ordered that he be charged with irreligion and be crucified.

So the whole mass of the brethren came together, rich and poor, orphans and widows, capable and helpless, wishing to see Peter and to rescue him; and the people cried out irrepressibly with a single voice, 'What harm has Peter done, Agrippa? How has he injured you? Answer the Romans!' And others said, 'If this man dies, we must fear that the Lord will destroy us too.'

And when Peter came to the place [of execution] he quietened the people and said, 'You men, who are soldiers of Christ, men who set their hopes on Christ, remember the signs and wonders which you saw through me, remember the compassion of God, how many healings he has performed for you. Wait for him that shall come and reward everyone according to his deeds. And now do not be angry with Agrippa; for he is the servant of his father's influence; and this is to happen in any event, because the Lord has shown me what is coming. But why do I delay and not go to the cross?'

Then when he had approached and stood by the cross he began to say, 'O name of the cross, mystery that is concealed! O grace ineffable that is spoken in the name of the cross! O nature of man that cannot be parted from God! O love unspeakable and inseparable, that cannot be disclosed through unclean lips! I seize thee now, being come to the end of my release from here. I will declare thee, what thou art; I will not conceal the mystery of the cross that has long been enclosed and hidden from my soul. You who hope in Christ, for you the cross must not be this thing that is visible; for this [passion], like the passion of Christ, is something other than this which is visible. And now above all, since you who can hear, can [hear it] from me, who am at the last closing hour of my life, give ear; withdraw your souls from every outward sense and from all that appears but is not truly real; close these eyes of yours, close your ears, withdraw from actions that are outwardly seen; and you shall know the facts about Christ and the whole secret of your salvation. Let so much be said to you who hear as though it were unspoken. But it is time for you, Peter, to surrender your body to those who are taking it. Take it, then, you whose duty this is. I request you therefore, executioners, to crucify me head-downwards – in this way and no other. And the reason I will tell to those who hear.'

Convicted and condemned, despite the protests of the Christian congregation, Peter took farewell of his friends, greeted the cross and demanded to be executed upside down.

And when they had hanged him up in the way which he had requested, he began to speak again, saying 'Men whose duty it is to hear, pay attention to what I shall tell you at this very moment that I am hanged up. You must know the mystery of all nature, and the beginning of all things, how it came about. For the first man, whose likeness I have in [my] appearance, in falling head-downwards showed a manner of birth that was not so before; for it was dead, having no movement. He therefore, being drawn down – he who also cast his first beginning down to the earth –

established the whole of this cosmic system, being hung up as an image of the calling, in which he showed what is on the right hand as on the left, and those on the left as on the right, and changed all the signs of their nature, so as to consider fair those things that were not fair, and take those that were really evil to be good. Concerning this the Lord says in a mystery, "Unless you make what is on the right hand as what is on the left hand and what is on the left hand as what is on the right and what is above as what is below and what is behind as what is before, you will not recognize the kingdom." This conception, then, I have declared to you, and the form in which you see me hanging is a representation of that man who first came to birth. You then, my beloved, both those who hear [me] now and those who shall hear in time, must leave your former error and turn back again; for you should come up to the cross of Christ, who is the Word stretched out, the one and only, of whom the Spirit says, "For what else is Christ but the Word, the sound of God?" So that the Word is this upright tree on which I am crucified; but the sound is the cross-piece, the nature of man; and the nail that holds the cross-piece to the upright in the middle is the conversion [or turning point] and repentance of man.

'Since then thou hast made known and revealed these things to me, O Word of life, which name I have just given to the tree, I give thee thanks, not with these lips that are nailed fast, nor with the tongue, through which truth and falsehood issue forth, nor with this word that comes forth by the skill of physical nature; but I give thee thanks, O King, with that voice which is known in silence, which is not heard aloud, which does not come forth through the bodily organs, which does not enter the ears of the flesh, that is not heard by corruptible substance, that is not in the world or uttered upon earth, nor is written in books, nor belongs to one but not to another; but with this [voice], Jesu Christ I thank thee, with silence of the voice, with which the spirit within me, that loves thee and speaks to thee and sees thee, makes intercession. Thou art known to the spirit only. Thou art my Father, thou art my Mother, thou my Brother, thou art Friend, thou art Servant, thou art House-keeper; thou art the All, and the All is in thee; thou art Being, and there is nothing that is, except thou.

'With him then do you also take refuge, brethren, and learning that in him alone is your real being, you shall obtain those things of which he says to you, "What eye has not seen nor ear heard, nor has it entered the heart of man." We ask then, for that which thou hast promised to give us, O Jesus undefiled; we praise thee, we give thanks to thee and confess thee, and being yet men without strength we glorify thee; for thou art God alone and no other, to whom be glory both now and for all eternity, Amen.'

But as the crowd that stood by shouted Amen with a resounding cry, at that very Amen, Peter gave up his spirit to the Lord.

Peter explained his request. Adam fell from grace headlong, as in an un-natural birth symbolizing a reversal of human values. But the supernatural kingdom or rule of God is only to be found by those who *will* reverse, will turn upside-down, will turn back-to-front the values of this natural world. Man can only come to God by penitence. The cross-beam can only be transfixed to the upright by the nail of penitence, and it is on the nail of penitence that the cross-beam can be converted and turned.

St Peter
and the Keys,
a cameo
by Cruelli.

Galilean fishermen holding the drag net.

4 James and John, Sons of Zebedee

With ten large townships encircling the Lake of Galilee and the further ten townships of the Greco-Roman Decapolis, there was a vast demand for fresh fish and consequently a thriving fishing industry on the lake. Fish were also pickled or cured at Tarichae, Capernaum and other centres, then packed in barrels to be transported by camel and donkey to Jerusalem and Samaria. Quantities of fish would be needed at the great feasts by the multitudes of pilgrims to the temple. Consequently the larger fishing concerns would have their own offices and representatives in Jerusalem, if not their branches in the coastal cities of Caesarea and Joppa. It is not therefore surprising to find the brothers of Bethsaida, Jonah and sons, in partnership with Zebedee and sons.

Indeed the very methods of fishing demanded the use of more than one fishing smack. The amateurs might use hook and line, or cast a drop-net into the shallows near the shore, but the bulk of fish required to supply such a demand could only be caught by very professional use of the drag-net and the deep-net.

The drag-net, which Arabs call 'the broom' because it sweeps the bottom of the lake, was loaded in coils into the stern of one boat, usually at dawn. The boat then set out in a huge arc or circle, the net being paid out from the stern as she moved forward. A second boat would secure the opposite end of the net until it was fully extended and the arc was complete. Both then made for the shore, dragging a considerable area before the ends of the net reached the willing hands on the beach ready to haul in the net. As the net sweeps slowly in, the shoal is encircled and the drag-net hardly holds the jumping fish, which have to be gathered into baskets by hand. When the ends of the net are joined the last of the catch is enclosed in a fold of net and dragged ashore, to be sorted and weighed out between the partners. Jesus used the illustration of the drag-net: 'Again, the kingdom of heaven is like a net which was thrown into the sea and gathered fish of every kind; when it was full, men drew it ashore and sat down and sorted the good into vessels but threw away the bad' (Matt. 13:47–48).

Fishing boats on the Sea of Galilee.

The deep-sea fishing, of which Peter was the mastermind, often depended upon the co-operation of the partners. This method involved an instinctive location of shoals at night, an accurate assessment of their movement and considerable skill in containing and netting them. The fish had on occasion to be attracted to the surface by a light suspended over the stern of each boat. Peter would certainly realize the forlorn hope of trawling in broad daylight, yet Jesus asked him to do just this, against his professional experience and better judgement. Peter obeyed with astonishing results, not only for himself but also the sons of Zebedee.

And when he had ceased speaking, he said to Simon, 'Put out into the deep and let down your nets for a catch.' And Simon answered, 'Master, we toiled all night and took nothing! But at your word I will let down the nets.' And when they had done this, they enclosed a great shoal of fish; and as their nets were breaking, they beckoned to their partners in the other boat to come and help them. And they came and filled both the boats, so that they began to sink. But when Simon Peter saw it, he fell down at Jesus' knees, saying, 'Depart from me, for I am a sinful man, O Lord.' For he was astonished, and all that were with him, at the catch of fish which they had taken; and so also were James and John, sons of Zebedee, who were partners with Simon. And Jesus said to Simon, 'Do not be afraid; henceforth you will be catching men.' And when they had brought their boats to land, they left everything and followed him (Luke 5:4–11).

The partnership of the brothers of Bethsaida and the sons of Zebedee was as necessary for their safety as their success. One of the most powerful factors in the lives of the Galilean fishermen still is the prevailing west wind, which seems to reach the lake from the Mediterranean in the early afternoon. On the west of the lake just above Magdala is the Gulf of Pigeons, running up to the Horns of Hattin (the site of the Crusader defeat in July 1187). The west wind funnels down through the gap across the flat plain of Gennesaret and soon whips up the surface of the lake, whose waves in winter can break upon the shore in spray ten feet high. At such times the presence of partners in another boat can make the difference between life and death; a storm on the lake can be a terrifying experience. As Dalman wrote in his *Sacred Sites and Ways*, 'the sailors fear the west wind, which may suddenly descend upon the lake, even at midday. Oftimes they will rest upon their oars to hear whether it is not already discernible above, on the heights, before it comes down.'

The fishermen disciples of Jesus were far from all being poor, simple, rustic peasants. Zebedee and his family were of some substance and status, of considerable skill and business acumen. He employed a hired crew and had at least one sizable smack for deep-sea fishing. Zebedee also allowed and enabled his wife Salome to give financial help towards the keep of Jesus and the twelve. He may possibly himself have been a disciple along with his

JAMES AND JOHN, SONS OF ZEBEDEE

AMBVLANS IHC IVXTA MARE GALILEAE·
VIDIT DVOS FRS· PETRVM ET ANDREAM ET
VOCAVIT EOS· AT ILLI RELICTIS RETIBVS SECV
TI SVNT EVM·

ET PCEDENS INDE· VIDIT ALIOS
DVOS FRS· IACOBVM ET IOHANNE
CVM ZEBEDEO PATRE· ET VOCAVIT
EOS· ET RELICTIS RETIBVS ET PATRE
SECVTI SVNT EVM

An 11th-century illustration, in a German Bible, shows Jesus calling Simon and
Andrew (on the left), James and John (on the right).

two sons, first of John the Baptist and then of Jesus.

A particularly interesting possibility is that the firm of 'Zebedee and
sons, of Galilee' was contracted to supply fish to the high priest's palace in
Jerusalem. A bishop of Ephesus at the end of the second century, named
Polycrates, described John as 'a witness and a teacher, who reclined upon the
bosom of the Lord, and who was a priest wearing the priestly diadem'. John's
priestly connection would help to account for the welcome of John-bar-
Zebedee, at the trial of Jesus, by the portress at the high priest's courtyard.

88

'Simon Peter followed Jesus and so did another disciple. As this disciple was known to the high priest, he entered the court of the high priest along with Jesus, while Peter stood outside at the door' (John 18:15–16).

In support of this, an apocryphal Gospel to the Nazaraeans, attributed to Matthew, is cited in a fourteenth-century German manuscript as giving the reason why John was known to the high priest: 'As he was the son of the poor fisherman Zebedee, he had often brought fish to the palace of the high priests Annas and Caiaphas. And John went out to the damsel that kept the door and secured from her permission for his companion Peter, who stood weeping loudly before the door, to come in.' This theory is further supported by a traditional site, in the upper city of Jerusalem, of the 'Fish shop of Zebedee', on which the Crusaders built a little cruciform church, now occupied by an Arab coffee house.

It is not unlikely that the brothers of Bethsaida and the sons of Zebedee were thus linked in a partnership involving the packing, transport, distribution and even sale of their catch. They constituted a co-operative that might well have employed most of the other members of the twelve. Unlike Peter and Andrew, however, James and John had a close familial link both with Jesus and even with John the Baptist. The mothers of James and John, and of Jesus, were the two sisters Salome and Mary, daughters of Joachim and Anna. That made them first-cousins of Jesus and relatives of John the Baptist, Jesus's cousin. The significance of family relationship in Jewish thinking and its influence on the foundation and progress of the Christian movement has not yet been fully grasped. The fact that the first leader of the Christian Church in Jerusalem was not one of the apostles, not even Peter himself, but James 'the brother of the Lord' is a remarkable indication of what a family affair the beginning of Christianity was.

The call of the sons of Zebedee seems to have happened very near both in time and place to the call of the brothers of Bethsaida, even though all four may have been with Jesus and his cousin John at the fords of the Jordan. 'And going on a little farther, he saw James the son of Zebedee and John his brother, who were in their boat mending the nets. And immediately he called them; and they left their father Zebedee in the boat with the hired servants, and followed him. And they went into Capernaum' (Mark 1:19–21).

After healing and teaching in the synagogue Jesus went with the four men to Simon Peter's house, which was to become the headquarters of the movement in Galilee.

James and John are next mentioned among the twelve called by Jesus from among his large following of disciples. At that time Jesus nicknamed the two brothers 'Boanerges', an Aramaic term meaning 'sons of thunder' and presumably referring either to their angry temperaments or glowering faces. Whether the nickname implies honour or rebuke, it is certain that

The call of the sons of Zebedee, who left their father and crew to follow Jesus – a painting by Edward Armitage.

John and sometimes his brother too were reproved by Jesus. John once said to Jesus at Capernaum, 'Master, we saw a man who is not one of us casting out devils in your name; and because he was not one of us we tried to stop him.' But Jesus said, 'You must not stop him: no one who works a miracle in my name is likely to speak evil of me. Anyone who is not against us is for us.'

When James and John asked Jesus to reserve the seats of honour on either side of him at his Messianic kingdom in heaven, Jesus replied, 'You do not know what you are asking.' And he went on to ask if they could share his destiny. They confidently affirmed that they could, whereupon Jesus answered, 'The cup that I must drink you shall drink . . . but as for the seats at my right hand or my left, these are not mine to grant. . . .' John and James received a further rebuke from Jesus when his messengers were not wel-

The raising of Jairus's daughter, in the presence of her parents, and of Peter, James and John. A 14th-century mosaic in the Kariye Camii Church, Istanbul.

James-bar-Zebedee on trial before Herod Agrippa, by Mantegna, in the church of the
Augustinian Order of Solitaries, at Padua.

comed in a Samaritan village, and the 'sons of thunder' suggested, perhaps typically, 'Lord, do you want us to call down fire from heaven to burn them up?' Jesus and his disciples shared the rigours of his itinerant ministry, often forced to go without shelter: 'The Son of Man has nowhere to lay his head'.

Despite their temperament and Jesus's frank rebukes, the two brothers, James and John, together with Peter, formed an inner circle within the group of disciples and it is these three whom Jesus took with him on at least three important occasions. They accompanied him into the house for the raising of Jairus's daughter; they were permitted to witness the glory of Jesus's Transfiguration on the mountain; and they were chosen to support him and to witness his agony in the Garden of Gethsemane.

Some scholars have seen in the name Boanerges a title exactly equivalent to 'the heavenly twins', Castor and Pollux, the sons of Zeus the Sky-god, who sit on each side of him as the 'children of the sky' controlling thunder and lightning. The name may have been just a playful allusion on the part of Jesus to their duality in appearance or conduct; the sons of Zebedee were not actually known to be twins but the possibility must not be discounted.

Barely fifteen years after their calling by the lakeside, James became the political victim of Herod Agrippa I, being executed shortly before Agrippa's own death. 'About that time Herod the king laid violent hands upon some who belonged to the church. He killed James the brother of John with the sword; and when he saw that it pleased the Jews, he proceeded to arrest Peter also' (Acts 12:1–3). James's martyrdom, described in a single sharp sentence of seven Greek words, is the only absolutely reliable (and the only biblical) record of the death of any one of the twelve apostles. James was also the first to drink his master's cup of death and to be baptized with his master's baptism of suffering, as his master had promised him (Mark 10:35–40).

There is no further scriptural reference to James son of Zebedee and there appears to have been some confusion in the minds of later writers between the two Jameses, the one being the cousin and the other the brother of Jesus. They are, however, clearly identified by Clement (in his Sixth Book of Institutions): 'Peter, James and John, after the Ascension of our Saviour, though they had been prepared by our Lord, did not contend for the honour, but chose James the Just as Bishop of Jerusalem.'

Eusebius further clarified the situation: 'There were, however, two Jameses; one called the Just, who was thrown from a wing of the Temple and beaten to death with a fuller's club. Another (James son of Zebedee) was beheaded.' Paul also mentions James the Just in his epistles: 'But I saw none of the other apostles except James the Lord's brother' (Gal. 1:19).

Outside the New Testament, James son of Zebedee is scarcely mentioned except in the Acts of John, the *Institutions* of Clement of Alexandria and the *Ecclesiastical History* of Eusebius, who quotes Clement. He,

A primitive illustration of the execution of St James.

Clement, relates a tradition received from his predecessors about James, 'that [the soldier] who led him to the law court, moved by his firm confession, confessed himself a Christian. They were now both led away, he relates, and on the way he begged that James would forgive his sins. After a brief consideration he said: Peace be with thee! and kissed him. After this both were beheaded at the same time.' Eusebius continues to refer to Herod Agrippa's arrest of Peter and Agrippa's subsequent sudden attack of dysentery and his death. On the other hand, an early psalm book refers to a stoning rather than a beheading of James.

A more recent tradition links James with the north-west coast of Spain. It was accepted until the sixteenth century throughout medieval Christendom that James had preached Christianity in Spain. The story goes that during his mission there, Mary the mother of Jesus, while still living, was miraculously transported, accompanied by angels bearing a marble pillar, to the banks of the river Ebro, that she talked with St James and told him to build a church dedicated to herself on the site where the pillar had been placed. The site is now the basilica of Nuestra Senora del Pilar at Saragossa. The legend continues that after his execution in Jerusalem, the apostle's body was taken to Galicia in north-west Spain and buried at a place where now stands the Cathedral of Santiago de Compostela, and that, in the ninth century, St James appeared on earth and helped the Spanish army to win a decisive victory over the Moors. The Santiago creed still remains an active element in Spanish religious life today.

Although James is the patron saint of Spain, and Iago a popular Spanish name, any historical connection between James and Spain in the brief decade or so between Pentecost and his martyrdom is almost impossible. The third-century apostolic history of Abdias (4: 1–9) tells of the conversion by James of two magicians. The first, called Philetus, after hearing the preaching of James, decided to leave his colleague Hermogenes; the latter, however, bound Philetus by magic. James, to whom Philetus appealed for help, secured his release. Hermogenes then sent diabolical agents to bring both James and Philetus to him; James, however, prevailed upon them to go and fetch the magician Hermogenes to him. This contest of magical strength ended with a victory for James, who released Hermogenes. He went back to his home, destroyed his books of magical art and returned to James to sue for pardon. The story closes with James sending him 'to undo his former work on those whom he had deceived, and to spend in charity what he had gained by his art'. He obeyed and so grew in faith that he too performed miracles.

The Santiago legend links these two erstwhile magicians with the taking of James's body by ship from Joppa to Spain. They landed at Iria Flavia, now known as El Padron, where James's body caused a series of wonderful miracles, but was lost in the barbarian invasions of the eighth century. Rediscovered in the following century by King Alphonso, the body was taken

The 11th-century cathedral, with an 18th-century baroque façade by Fernando de Casal, at Santiago de Compostela, north-west Spain.

to Compostela, where tradition says it still remains. The name 'Compostela' is probably a conflation of the Spanish term *'Giacomo Postolo'*, James the Apostle. The Virgin Mary is supposed to have appeared to James at Saragossa. The whole story probably dates from the seventh-century works of Isadore of Seville.

It is unfortunate that although James was one of the inner circle of three among the apostles there is so little factual information about him. His was the shortest ministry and his younger brother's was perhaps the longest. A Roman coin engraved with two oxen, the one facing an altar and the other a plough, well illustrates the respective destinies of these two sons of Zebedee. The coin bears the inscription 'Ready for either', the brief moment of sacrifice or the long furrow; and so indeed the sons of Zebedee 'drank the cup' of their master, Jesus (Mark 10:35–39).

The character of both the two brothers that emerges clearly from the first three Gospels is that both were men of considerable ambition, of explosive temper and intolerant heart. There is little more information within the synoptic Gospels about John than about his brother. Two further references are made to John during the last day or so before the Crucifixion of Jesus. 'And as he sat on the Mount of Olives opposite the temple, Peter and James and John and Andrew asked him privately, "Tell us, when will this be, and what will be the sign when these things are all to be accomplished?"' (Mark 13:3–4). 'So Jesus sent Peter and John, saying, "Go and prepare the passover for us, that we may eat it"' (Luke 22:8).

Within the Acts of the Apostles, John is shown as a partner with Peter in the active leadership of the twelve in the period after Pentecost. Together the two apostles constantly preached and healed in the temple area at Jerusalem.

Now Peter and John were going up to the temple at the hour of prayer, the ninth hour. And a man lame from birth was being carried, whom they laid daily at that gate of the temple which is called Beautiful to ask alms of those who entered the temple. Seeing Peter and John about to go into the temple, he asked for alms. And Peter directed his gaze at him, with John, and said, 'Look at us.' And he fixed his attention upon them, expecting to receive something from them. But Peter said, 'I have no silver and gold, but I give you what I have; in the name of Jesus Christ of Nazareth, walk.' And he took him up by the right hand and raised him up; and immediately his feet and ankles were made strong. And leaping up he stood and walked and entered the temple with them, walking and leaping and praising God. And all the people saw him walking and praising God, and recognized him as the one who sat for alms at the Beautiful Gate of the temple; and they were filled with wonder and amazement at what had happened to him. While he clung to Peter and John, all the people ran together to them in the portico called Solomon's, astounded (Acts 3:1–11).

PREVIOUS PAGES St James and St John among the Twelve Apostles in the 12th-century mural at Eski Gumus, Turkey. James, the elder brother, appears darker and younger than John.

A Raphael cartoon of the healing of the lame man by Peter and John at the Beautiful Gate of the Temple in Jerusalem.

These two drew the attention of the Sanhedrin by the success of their bold and powerful preaching:

And as they were speaking to the people, the priests and the captain of the temple and the Sadducees came upon them, annoyed because they were teaching the people and proclaiming in Jesus the resurrection from the dead. And they arrested them and put them in custody until the morrow, for it was already evening. But many of those who heard the word believed; and the number of the men came to about five thousand (Acts 4:1–4).

Despite the scarcity of scripture references specifically to John son of Zebedee, there may well be another source of information. For it is possible that John may have been the person referred to in the Fourth Gospel as 'the beloved disciple'. If so, then a very great deal more of his character and the important part played by him in the Upper Room, at Calvary, at the empty tomb, and in Galilee can be seen. Such an identification would, however, presuppose some change of character in John during his association with Jesus. The rather immature young 'son of thunder' would need to have become a lovable and highly perceptive personality.

The term 'the disciple Jesus loved' is used only by the writer of the

Fourth Gospel and on only four occasions, all during or following the Passion of Jesus. The first scene is set in the Upper Room on the night of the Last Supper, after the meal. Jesus, having washed the disciples' feet, sat down with them and warned them of his forthcoming betrayal. 'Truly, truly, I say to you, one of you will betray me.' The disciples looked at each other, wondering who it could be. 'The disciple whom Jesus loved' was reclining next to Jesus. Simon Peter signed to him and said, 'Tell us who it is of whom he speaks'; so leaning back on Jesus's breast he said, 'Lord, who is it?' 'It is he to whom I shall give a morsel when I have dipped it.' He dipped the piece of bread and gave it to Judas.

The second occasion is on Calvary when the Crucifixion is completed and the long agony has begun. 'When Jesus saw his mother, and the disciple whom he loved standing near, he said to his mother, "Woman, behold your son!" Then he said to the disciple, "Behold your mother!" And from that hour the disciple took her to his own home,' traditionally on the Western Hill.

The third occasion when the term was used is early on Easter morning when Mary of Magdala has been to the tomb only to find it empty and the stone rolled away. 'So she ran, and went to Simon Peter and the other disciple, the one whom Jesus loved, and said to them, "They have taken the Lord out of the tomb . . .".' So Peter set out with the other disciple. They ran together, but the other disciple, running faster than Peter, reached the tomb first; he bent down and saw the linen cloths lying on the ground but did not go in. Peter who was following now came up, went first into the tomb, saw the linen cloths there and also the cloth that had been over the head rolled up in a place by itself. 'Then the other disciple, who reached the tomb first, also went in, and he saw and believed. . . .'

The final scene is some time later on the Lake of Galilee after a fruitless night's fishing with Peter and the others. As they bring the boat into the north shore, a voice calls, 'Cast the net on the right side' (to starboard). They do so and enclose so vast a haul of fish that they cannot even land it. At that moment 'that disciple whom Jesus loved' said to Peter: 'It is the Lord!' After landing the catch and eating breakfast on the beach, Peter is solemnly thrice commissioned by Jesus to feed his sheep. Then Jesus predicts Peter's own destiny of crucifixion: '"When you are old, you will stretch out your hands, and another will gird you and carry you where you do not wish to go." And after this he said to him, "Follow me." Peter turned and saw following them the disciple whom Jesus loved, who had lain close to his breast at the supper . . . and said to Jesus, "Lord, what about this man?" Jesus said to him, "If it is my will that he remain until I come, what is that to you? Follow me!"' The closing verses or epilogue of the Gospel state: 'This is the disciple who is bearing witness to these things, and who has written these things; and we know that his testimony is true.'

The Crucifixion of Jesus between the two thieves, by Johan Holbein, depicts Mary his mother and John-bar-Zebedee at the foot of the cross.

From these four scenes it seems inconceivable that this intimate friend should have been outside the twelve, if even outside the inner circle of Peter, James and John. Apart from the list of fishermen on this final expedition in the last chapter of the Gospel, there is not a single reference to John, son of Zebedee. It is unlikely that a disciple so often mentioned within the other three Gospels should be unconsciously omitted from the Fourth Gospel, even though he was often rebuked! It is likely that John, son of Zebedee, was the 'disciple Jesus loved', even if the Gospel of John was written by another hand.

It must have been the work of someone whose affection and respect for John, son of Zebedee, was considerable and who was willing to undersign all he said. In fact the authority for the Gospel is that of John, son of Zebedee, even if the authorship is not.

Whoever the actual author of the Fourth Gospel was, the depth and the effect of his work places him second in importance only to Paul among the members of the primitive Christian Church. It was this man who, writing in the very last years of the first century when all eye-witnesses to the life of Jesus were dead, expressed a wonderful union between the belief in an historical outward act of God and a living inward experience of the risen Jesus. His book is a meditation in the manner of the Jewish *Midrash*, but in Christian form. In parts it is very early indeed, especially the narrative of the Passion of Jesus. It has affinities too with the Qumran literature of the Dead Sea Scrolls and may perhaps have been based on a Palestinian Aramaic original, now lost.

As to who did in fact write the Fourth Gospel, internal evidence appears to identify the author with John, son of Zebedee, particularly the four passages concerning 'the disciple Jesus loved'. By a process of elimination it can be confirmed that this phrase refers to John, son of Zebedee, who is not otherwise mentioned in the Gospel, except perhaps as the companion of Peter and the disciple of John the Baptist. If John, son of Zebedee, is the author, however, 'the disciple Jesus loved' is a strangely immodest title for an author to apply to himself. If, however, the Gospel had been dictated to scribes, in the first person, they could have replaced the words 'I, John' with 'the disciple whom Jesus loved'. Were the actual author to be other than John, son of Zebedee, from whom, however, the information was received, such a title would be possible. Were the actual author to have respected John, son of Zebedee, as being loved by Jesus more openly than the other disciples, such a title would be understandable. Now, the final appendix to the Gospel specifically identifies the authority for the Gospel with the 'disciple Jesus loved' and therefore with John, son of Zebedee. These verses also imply that the actual author was himself a disciple of John, son of Zebedee.

The external evidence at first appears conflicting; some of the early

Fathers of the Church, such as Irenaeus of Lyons (130–200) and Clement of Rome (*c.* 100), argued for John, son of Zebedee, as the author when at Ephesus. However, Papias, bishop of Hieropalis (60–130), said that there were *two* Johns, the apostle who was dead and the elder who was still alive. Dionysius, a later bishop of Ephesus, confirmed that there were two tombs at Ephesus, both ascribed to a John. In any case, a strong tradition connected the Gospel with Ephesus. The conclusion seems to be again that the authority for this Gospel was that of John, son of Zebedee, but that it was either written or edited by an elder, also living at Ephesus and also called John. The second and third letters of John are both addressed from 'the Elder' and are probably the work of this second John. The first letter resembles, more than the second and third, the style and content of the Gospel and may therefore be the work of John, son of Zebedee.

The Fourth Gospel was written at the end of the apostolic age, before the turn of the first century, when there were no longer eye-witnesses to the life of Jesus to inspire and proclaim, except perhaps the aged John. The primitive hopes and momentum were spent; moreover Christianity had to be adapted to the needs of the Hellenistic world. Christianity had to unite her belief in an historical act of God with her present inward experience. John set out to fulfil two objects, one purely religious, the other practical.

First, he set out to impress the belief that Jesus was not only the Messiah and the Son of Man of Jewish tradition, but also the Son of God – a title more understandable and far more significant to the pagan world. Men must 'believe' in the actual historic person of Jesus and 'have life' by a realization of the purpose of his life, which is not merely a thing of the past but an ever-living fact of the present. Jesus's life on earth was only the beginning of a larger and ever-enduring life open to all believers; for the historical person of Jesus could be revealed to any true believer, now and always. Secondly, John had a practical object – to meet some of the questions and accusations levelled at Christianity by his pagan contemporaries and to support and build up the idea of the Christian Church.

John himself had a strong and certain conception of both the person and the life of Christ, and not unnaturally interpreted facts accordingly. To him, facts were valuable because they supported or illustrated the beliefs he wanted to impress. He therefore selected and concentrated upon a few episodes which bear witness to the divinity of Christ. Similarly, he adapted and modified his selected material, reading a meaning into words and incidents independent of their actual circumstances. To him the outward event was often a mere shell, covering a hidden message, which was only apparent to the believer.

Consequently John did not, like Mark, record by narrative and dialogue events as they happened; he adapted and matched narrative to dialogue, and vice versa, to achieve his purpose. Therefore both narrative and dialogue are in the same style and it is sometimes impossible to distinguish editorial comment from narrative or dialogue. The teaching of Jesus, combined with editorial comment, makes up long discourses. Through the calculated combination of narratives and discourses, John adapted to the needs of his readers the Gospel message, as it was recorded by Mark or as he, John, had seen and heard it.

John sought to interpret the Jewish ideas of 'Messiah' and 'kingdom' in such terms as 'truth' and 'eternal life'. This is well illustrated in the private conversation at the trial in which Pilate asked Jesus, 'Are you the King of the Jews?' (Messiah). 'Jesus answered, "My kingship is not of this world . . .". Pilate said to him, "So you are a king?" Jesus answered, "You say that I am a king. For this I was born and for this I have come into the world, to bear witness to the truth. Every one who is of the truth hears my voice."'

The prologue – the first eighteen verses of the Fourth Gospel – is a poem about the 'Word' of God. John opens his prologue as the Book of Genesis. The Greek words 'In the beginning' can equally mean 'In principle' or 'At the root of the universe' – thus implying not just an event in time but also an eternal reality: 'In the beginning was the Word, and the Word was with God, and the Word was God. He was in the beginning with God; all things were made through him, and without him was not anything made that was made. In him was life, and the life was the light of men. The light shines in the darkness, and the darkness has not overcome it.' The writer identified Jesus with the *Logos* or 'Word' of God. Mark began his Gospel with John the Baptist. John began the Fourth Gospel with the Creation. The Gospel was uttered in the 'Word' of God, but Jesus was and is the Gospel and the 'Word' that began the creation of the Word itself. The *Logos* was no new thing. It existed before creation. The world in its entirety was his creation. The psalmist wrote: 'By the word of the Lord the heavens were made and all their host' (Ps. 33). So the Gospel concerned all men. It was the light of all men. It was identical with the author of life, but it was rejected and the darkness did not understand it, nor indeed quench it. He was, to John, both the creative word and the very presence of God.

The first letter of John within the New Testament opens with a similar sort of preface to that of the Gospel, using similar words such as 'the beginning' and the *Logos*. In this preface the writer declares the purpose of his letter. The body of the letter consists of three clear and simple expositions: on the nature of Christianity, life in the family of God, and the certainty of the Christian faith. The letter ends with a brief postscript and an encouragement to prayer. From the second century the traditional view has been that John, son of Zebedee, was the author of the Gospel and of the letters of John. Only in recent years has the identification of authorship been challenged. The styles of the Gospel and the first letter are similar. A list has

St John, exiled to the Island of Patmos, recorded his visions in the Book of Revelation – oil-painted wood panel by the Flemish artist Joos van Cleve, *c.* 1525.

been compiled of at least fifty phrases in the first letter which have close parallels in the Gospel. Both use the method of antithesis, or contrast, of darkness and light, flesh and spirit, truth and falsehood. The first letter of John claims to have been written by an eye-witness who has 'seen, heard, and handled' Jesus, the 'Word' of God. Even if the Gospel might not have been the work of the apostle, John, son of Zebedee, there is no reason why the first letter should not have been.

Both the second-century scholars Papias and Irenaeus considered that the author of both Gospel and letters had been 'a disciple of the Lord', a survivor of the group who had actually followed Jesus in his lifetime, who had lived on into the reign of Trajan – to an age of ninety years or more. If John, son of Zebedee, did live to this age, it is just possible that he was also the Seer of Patmos, whose visions are recorded in the Book of Revelation. This would depend, however, upon the truth of two somewhat contra-

The death of the Virgin Mary, by the Master of Cologne.

The gate in the east wall of the Old City, Jerusalem, built by the 13th-century Sultan Beibars and bearing his hallmark, the lions, but called by the Arabs 'the Gate of the Lady Mary'.

OVERLEAF Mantegna's painting of Christ at prayer in the Garden of Gethsemane. His inner circle Peter, James and John sleep, while the rabble approaches from the city.

dictory traditions, one that John remained in Jerusalem or Judaea, the other that he travelled the eastern Mediterranean and died at Ephesus.

The Fourth Gospel tells of the words from the cross, by which Jesus consigned his mother Mary and his beloved disciple John to each other's care: 'Woman, behold your son!' and 'Behold your mother!' The writer then affirms that 'from that hour the disciple took her to his own home' (19:25–27). If, in fact, their lives from that moment were inextricably linked, then the whereabouts of Mary may well provide the clue to the location of John's own ministry. Here again, however, there are two clearly contrary theories or traditions as to where Mary lived her last years. One is that she remained in Jerusalem to live in the house of John bar Zebedee, traditionally on Mount Zion. The other is that she accompanied John to Ephesus, where she lived to the end of her life. Both theories are supported by local tradition.

In Jerusalem, Mary is venerated by Christians and Muslims and respected by Jews. The eastern gate into the Old City is called in Arabic *Bab Sitt Mariam*, the 'Gate of the Lady Mary'. The area inside and outside that part of the city has long been associated with Mary. East of the viaduct on which the Jericho road crosses the Kedron is an ancient church, now almost buried by the accumulation of centuries of rubble in the bottom of the ravine. A tradition records how the body of Mary, the mother of Jesus, was brought here from the house of John on Mount Zion for burial. An extension of this same tradition records how from here she was carried bodily into heaven, three days after her burial.

The Church in the Byzantine Empire, including Ephesus, seems to have accepted this tradition before 787, and Ephesus as the place of Mary's burial has very little traditional support. From Byzantine times, a large church on the Western Hill, called 'Christian Zion', was said to cover several sites. These included the Upper Room and place of feet-washing, later to become the first synagogue of the Christian community, the house of John, and later also the place of the supposed 'falling asleep' of Mary.

The Ephesian theory, on the other hand, is that following the early persecutions, the diaspora of Hellenistic Christians, and Peter's departure from Jerusalem, John took Mary the mother of Jesus to Anatolia, on the west coast of Asia Minor. Paul's failure to mention John's or Mary's presence in Ephesus is sometimes put forward as an objection to this theory, but it must be pointed out that he also made no mention of Peter's mission to Rome, although Peter died there before Paul.

The dedication of the basilica at Ephesus to Haghia Maria in the fourth century, at a time when dedications were only made because of the presence of relics, is taken as evidence of the residence of Mary. The two great councils of 431 and 449 were held in this vast building.

In the fifth century, Pope Celestine I referred to Ephesus as the home of

Despite its Crusader portico, the Tomb of Mary in the Kedron Ravine appeared on the 6th-century Madeba mosaic map of Jerusalem.

Greco-Roman remains at Ephesus, a gateway at the top of the street of the Curetes, a college of priests attached to the service of Artemis.

Mary the mother of Jesus and of John. Hippolytus of Thebes in the seventh century mentioned that Mary had lived for eleven years at Ephesus before her death. This tradition survived the Muslim occupation of Ephesus in 1090 and thrived among the scattered Christian community in surrounding villages. Since the end of the last century, a small shrine in the Byzantine style, some miles to the south of the ruins of Ephesus, has been a place of Latin pilgrimage and devotion, as symbolizing a home of Mary in Ephesus. The discovery of this 'house' was the direct result of the visions of an eighteenth-century German mystic, Catherine Emmeric, who had never visited Ephesus! The preponderance, however, of scholarly opinion and archaeological evidence supports the third-century tradition of Mary's life and death in Jerusalem rather than in Ephesus.

The Fathers of the Church present apparently contradictory traditions. The eighth-century Patriarch of Constantinople, Nicephorus, stated that John had stayed in Jerusalem and cared for Mary like a son until the day of

The house of the Virgin Mary at Ephesus, a shrine in the Byzantine style, on a traditional site of her last home with St John.

her death. The Carthaginian lawyer Tertullian (*c.* 160–220), and the fourth-century Roman biblical scholar Jerome, insisted that John had gone to Rome, where he had survived being thrown into a cauldron of boiling oil and being forced to drink a cup of hemlock poison. Irenaeus and Eusebius related that John was imprisoned on the island of Patmos and then went to Ephesus.

The Ephesian tradition is, however, followed with conviction and detail in both the Acts of John and in the *Ecclesiastical History* of Eusebius. The Acts, known to Clement of Alexandria, must have originated around the year 150 in the province of Asia, where the memory of John remained vividly clear. Eusebius stated that when the apostles scattered Asia was allotted to John and that he died at Ephesus. Only three sizable fragments of the Acts remain. They tell of John's journeys to Rome before the reign of Domitian but do not mention the story of the boiling cauldron. They speak of his exile to Patmos, his miracles at Ephesus, a visit to Laodicea. They include some novel material about the life and passion of Jesus and close with a report of the death and burial of the Apostle John. The Acts of John were written by Leucius Charinus, reputedly a disciple of the Apostle John. Massive collections of legends about the apostle appeared from the fifth century onwards. They went far beyond the original Acts of John and gained a wide circulation in the east but little credence in the west.

The Acts of John, about the same length as Matthew's Gospel, was originally written in Greek, though later expurgated versions appeared in Latin. There are two texts. In the first, the Emperor Domitian is reported to have heard of John's teaching in Ephesus and to have sent for him to Rome. On the journey his ascetic habits impressed his captors. Brought before Domitian he was forced to drink poison, which did him no harm but killed a criminal, whom John revived. John also raised a girl who had been killed by an evil spirit. Domitian was much impressed but banished John to Patmos and never recalled him.

The second text describes John's shipwreck on leaving Patmos, swimming on a cork buoy, until he landed at Miletus on the mainland, from where he went to Ephesus. The 'boiling oil' story appears to be linked with both Domitian in Rome and the proconsul at Ephesus, though the Romans fixed the place and the date, by the Festival of 'St John before the Latin Gate', on 6 May.

The Acts go on to relate the raising of Lycomedes, the praetor of Ephesus, and the healing of his sick wife, Cleopatra, the dedication and the destruction of the temple of Artemis, at Ephesus. This last story is incredible, considering the fact that Ephesus was the great city of paganism in Asia. Its temple of Diana was the centre of pagan worship for all the Mediterranean lands. The proud title of this great commercial and religious centre was 'Neocorus' – temple-keeper or sacristan – of Artemis. Consequently the temple of Artemis enjoyed the services of an army of virgin-prophetesses, eunuch-priests, choristers, vergers and even acrobats – in a spate of infamous and immoral excess. Ephesus – in the early Christian era – was a city of magic and necromancy, the home of a superstition so ancient and deeply rooted that it outlived the gods of Olympus.

The narrative of the Acts runs thus:

Now two days later there was the dedication-festival of the idol–temple. So while everyone was wearing white, John alone put on black clothing and went up to the temple; and they seized him and tried to kill him. But John said, 'You are mad to lay hands on me, a man who serves the one true God.' And he went up on a high platform, and said to them,

'Men of Ephesus, you are liable to behave like the sea; every river at its outfall, every spring that flows down, the rains and incessant waves and stony torrents, are all made salt by the bitter brine that is in it. You likewise have remained to this day unchanged [in your attitude] towards the true religion, and are being corrupted by

The boiling in oil and miraculous preservation of St John, in Rome under Domitian, is commemorated in the Western Church on 6 May, 'St John before the Latin Gate', Dürer.

your ancient rituals. How many miracles [and] cures of diseases have you seen [performed] through me? And yet you are blinded in your hearts, and cannot recover your sight. What is it then, men of Ephesus? I have ventured to come up now into this very idol-temple of yours, I will convict you of being utterly godless and dead through human reasoning. See, here I stand. You all say that you have Artemis as your goddess [or, that Artemis has power]; so pray in her [name] and I, and I alone, may die; or if you cannot do this, then I alone will call upon my own God and because of your unbelief I will put you all to death.'

And when John was saying this, of a sudden the altar of Artemis split into many pieces, and all the offerings laid up in the temple suddenly fell to the floor and its goodness was broken, and so were more than seven images; and half the temple fell down, so that the priest was killed at one stroke as the roof came down. Then the assembled Ephesians cried out, '[There is but] one God, [the God] of John!' And the people rising from the ground went running and threw down the rest of the idol temple, crying out, 'The God of John [is the] only [God] we know; from now on we worship him, since he has had mercy on us.'

Eusebius devotes a whole chapter (XXIII) to the Apostle John. On the accession of Nero to the imperial crown, the honours of Domitian were revoked and all those who had been unjustly exiled were restored. It was then also that the Apostle John returned from his banishment at Patmos and took up his abode at Ephesus, according to an ancient tradition of the Church.

About this time too, the beloved disciple of Jesus, John the apostle and evangelist, still surviving, governed the churches in Asia, after his return from exile on the island, and the death of Domitian. That he was living until this time may be proved by the testimony of two witnesses. These, as maintaining sound doctrine in the Church, may surely be regarded as worthy of all credit; and such were Irenaeus and Clement of Alexandria. Of these, the former, in the second book against heresies, writes in the following manner: 'And all the presbyters of Asia, that had conferred with John the disciple of our Lord, testify that John had delivered it to them; for he continued with them until the times of Trajan.' And in the third book of the same work, he shows the same thing in the following words: 'The church in Ephesus also, which had been founded by Paul, and where John continued to abide until the times of Trajan, is a faithful witness of the apostolic tradition.' Clement also, indicating the time, adds:

Listen to a story that is no fiction, but a real history, handed down and carefully preserved, respecting the Apostle John. For after the tyrant was dead, coming from the Isle of Patmos to Ephesus, he went also, when called, to the neighbouring regions of the Gentiles; in some to appoint bishops, in some to institute entire new churches, in others to appoint in the ministry some one of those that were pointed out by the Holy Ghost.

OPPOSITE ABOVE 'Diana or Christ?' by Alwin Long, depicts the choice facing early Christians of sacrificing to the gods of the state, or refusing on pain of death.

OPPOSITE BELOW Complex of remains at Ephesus. In the foreground the Temple of Artemis, beyond is the Basilica of St John, left skyline the Citadel, below this the Selcuk Mosque.

While visiting a certain congregation near Ephesus, John noticed a young man of 'fine stature, graceful countenance and ardent mind' whom he committed to the care of the local bishop before returning to Ephesus. The bishop educated and cared for him, but all too soon relaxed his vigilance and the young man fell into bad company, who seduced him and initiated him into their own thieves' kitchen. Soon the man became captain of his own robber band 'surpassing them all in violence, blood and cruelty'. When John revisited that church some time later, he astonished the bishop with these words:

'Come, bishop, return me my deposit, which I and Christ committed to thee, in the presence of the church over which thou dost preside. I demand the young man, and the soul of a brother.' The old man, groaning heavily and also weeping, said, 'He is dead.' 'How, and what death?' 'He is dead to God,' he said. 'He has turned out wicked and abandoned, and at last a robber; and now, instead of the church, he has beset the mountain with a band like himself.'

The apostle, on hearing this, tore his garment, and beating his head with great lamentation said, 'I left a fine keeper of a brother's soul! But let a horse now be got ready, and some one to guide me on my way.' He rode as he was, away from the church, and coming to the country, was taken prisoner by the outguard of the banditti. He neither attempted, however, to flee, nor refused to be taken; but cried out, 'For this very purpose am I come; conduct me to your captain.' He, in the meantime, stood waiting, armed as he was. But as he recognized John advancing towards him, overcome with shame he turned about to flee. The apostle, however, pursued him with all his might, forgetful of his age, and crying out, 'Why dost thou fly, my son, from me, thy father; thy defenceless, aged father? Have compassion on me, my son, fear not. Thou has still hope of life. I will intercede with Christ for thee. Should it be necessary, I will cheerfully suffer death for thee, as Christ for us. I will give my life for thine. Stay; believe Christ hath sent me.' Hearing this, he at first stopped with downcast looks; then threw away his arms; then trembling, lamented bitterly, and embracing the old man as he came up, attempted to plead for himself with his lamentations, as much as he was able; as if baptized a second time with his own tears, and only concealing his right hand. But the apostle pledging himself, and solemnly assuring him, that he had found pardon for him in his prayers at the hands of Christ, praying on his bended knees, and kissing his right hand as cleansed from all iniquity, conducted him back to the church.

There is something of the Boanerges spirit, despite John's maturity, in this story, something of both the anger and love of his Galilean friend and rabbi. Another glimpse of John's old age is given by Jerome (in his commentary on Galatians 6: 10).

When John tarried in Ephesus to extreme old age, and could only with difficulty be carried to the church in the arms of his disciples, and was unable to give utterance to many words, he used to say no more at their several meetings than this: 'Little children love one another.' At length the disciples and fathers who were there,

St John, a mural in the 18th-century church of St Onoufrios, Cyprus, where the four evangelists are depicted in the four central arches.

wearied with always hearing the same words, said: 'Master, why dost thou always say this?' 'It is the Lord's command,' was his reply, 'and, if this alone be done, it is enough.'

The same simplicity of life and love is reflected in the description of his end, his final prayer and farewell, in the Acts of John.

'And grant me to finish my way to thee preserved from violence and insult, receiving what thou hast promised to them that live purely and love thee alone.' And having sealed himself in every part, standing thus, he said '[Be] thou with me, Lord Jesus Christ'; and he lay down in the trench where he had spread out his clothes; and he said to us, 'Peace [be] with you, my brethren', and gave up his spirit rejoicing.

5 Philip and Bartholomew

The names of Philip and Bartholomew are inseparably linked in the Synoptic Gospels which, however, do no more than list their names. It is the Fourth Gospel which describes a number of incidents involving them both, from which some estimate of their characters and personalities may be deduced. There are problems concerning the identity of each man. There are two Philips in the early Christian Church, one specified as 'the apostle', the other variously called 'the deacon' or 'the evangelist'. From the second century many scholars have identified the two as one, but both, by function within their particular circle or grouping, might well have been termed 'provisioner'. The 'friend' appears under different names in the Synoptic and Fourth Gospels, being apparently called 'Nathaniel' by John and 'Bartholomew' by the others.

Nathaniel and Bartholomew may together form the personal name and patronymic of one and the same man. Nathaniel is from the Hebrew 'God has given', Bartholomew from the Greek form of the Aramaic 'Son of Tolmai'. Certainly whoever was called 'Son of Tolmai' must have had a personal name. In all three Synoptic Gospels Bartholomew is always linked with Philip. In the Fourth Gospel, in the first and last chapters, Nathaniel is introduced to Jesus by Philip and is then a witness together with Philip of his Resurrection. The name Nathaniel does not appear in the Synoptic Gospels, nor does the name Bartholomew appear in the Fourth Gospel. It seems only reasonable that these two names, intimately connected with Philip, do in fact refer to the same man, Nathaniel Bartholomew. This identification has been accepted by scholars since the ninth century.

The problem of the Philips is not so easily solved. To identify 'the apostle' and 'the deacon' as one man would seem on the face of it strangely illogical, considering that the deacons were ordained by the apostles specifically to relieve them of domestic duties. Yet this is exactly what Eusebius does in the early part of the third century. Moreover in doing so, he claims to be quoting a number of earlier scholars. Among these the earliest was Polycarp, bishop

Mosaics of Philip and Bartholomew, the provisioner of the twelve and his friend, the first an 11th-century mosaic from the monastery of Osios Loukas in Achaia, and the second from the 6th-century church of San Vitale, Ravenna.

of Smyrna, who was born about the year 70. Papias, the early second-century bishop of Hierapolis in Phrygia, knew Philip's daughters and their home in the city of Hierapolis. Irenaeus, his successor, and Polycrates, bishop of Ephesus in the second century, also identified the apostle with the deacon; Polycrates added that two of Philip's spinster daughters were buried at Hierapolis on either side of Philip himself, and that a third daughter was buried at Ephesus. Their graves, he said, could still be seen. Proclus, in the early third century, specifically identified the apostle with the deacon who had lived at Caesarea and had had four daughters. This was, or might have been, a very natural error, for Philip the Apostle also had daughters and had settled in Hierapolis in West Phrygia, an important city near Colossae and Laodicea. Coptic and Armenian liturgical calendars list a commemoration of Philip as both 'apostle and deacon'. Certainly if there were two men (and this is more likely), their varying activities soon became fused and confused in Jewish–Christian tradition.

Within the Gospels of Mark, Matthew and Luke, the name of Philip the Apostle occurs only in the list of apostles, linked with that of Nathaniel Bar-Tolmai. In the Acts, his name is listed with Thomas among the apostles present at the election of Matthias in the Upper Room before Pentecost. Philip was almost certainly a disciple of John the Baptist, because Jesus called him from among the crowds on the banks of the river Jordan where John was baptizing. The previous day, Jesus had met Andrew, who had introduced to Jesus his brother Simon Peter. All three of them – Andrew, Peter and Philip – came from the same town, Bethsaida, on the Lake of Galilee, and were fishermen. It was probably a day or two later that Philip brought his friend Nathaniel to Jesus.

The Fourth Gospel describes how Jesus was on the way back to Galilee from his own baptism by John the Baptist in the Jordan Valley. On his way, he passed through the village of Cana, where Nathaniel lived. His friend Philip called in to see Nathaniel and to say, 'We have found him of whom Moses in the law and also the prophets wrote, Jesus of Nazareth, the son of Joseph.' Nathaniel thought of Nazareth, the place up the road from Cana, as a rather insignificant and uncouth little town. 'Can anything good come out of Nazareth?' Philip said to him, 'Come and see.'

In the quaint little village of Cana, Nathaniel was an earnest and sincere Jew, who was looking forward to the coming of the Messiah. It was his custom, as it was of many orthodox Jews, to sit under the family fig-tree whenever he wished to be quiet and pray. Now it so happened that the day Philip went to bring him to Jesus, that is exactly what he had been doing. He had been reading about the patriarch Jacob and his cunning. He had been reading about the dream of the ladder and the angels going up and down between heaven and earth. Perhaps, too, he had read of Jacob wrestling with the angel and winning the name of 'Israel', which means 'who prevails with

God'. At any rate, he, Nathaniel, had begun to wrestle with the idea that this new teacher from Nazareth could be the long expected Messiah, for whom Philip and he had been waiting. So he said, 'Not from Nazareth, surely?' and Philip answered, 'Come and see,' and so they went. As Nathaniel approached, Jesus read his thoughts and said to him, 'Behold, an Israelite indeed, in whom is no guile!' Nathaniel was absolutely stunned and said, 'How do you know me?' Jesus answered, 'Before Philip called you, when you were under the fig-tree, I saw you.' That is, 'My sympathy had reached you, before your friend broke in with the news that confirmed your thoughts and prayers.' Nathaniel could only exclaim, 'Rabbi, you are the Son of God! You are the King of Israel!'

It is as though Jesus of Nazareth, here actually called by the title that was to be nailed to his cross, 'King of the Jews', again addressed Nathaniel along these lines: 'Are you believing because I saw you under the fig-tree? Is that why you believe? No, of course not! It is because of your honest wrestling with your doubts. You are a true son of Jacob. Now I promise you greater things. Jacob saw a ladder set up to heaven and "the angels of God ascending and descending on it". You will see heaven opened and the angels of God ascending and descending upon the Son of Man. Now you are looking at him of whom that ladder is just a picture. You see him who is the link between heaven and earth.'

Philip is next mentioned within the Fourth Gospel in the story of the Feeding of the Five Thousand, where he appears to have been responsible for the provisioning of the party of disciples, or for their picnic rations. Certainly he was staggered at the idea of feeding such a crowd, when Jesus suggested buying bread for them. Jesus may have turned instinctively to Philip, as in charge of the commissariat and Philip may have at once calculated the cost. 'Two hundred denarii would not buy enough for each of them to get a little,' Philip answered, perhaps with more simplicity than accuracy! No doubt he was as horrified as the others when Jesus said, 'Make the people sit down,' and equally astonished at the outcome.

During Jesus's final visit to Jerusalem before the Crucifixion, some Greeks had come up for the Passover. They approached Philip with the request, 'Sir, we wish to see Jesus.' Philip told Andrew and together they went to tell Jesus. Perhaps Philip again invited his enquirers to 'Come and see'.

Again, at the Last Supper, Philip's words to Jesus are recorded in the Fourth Gospel. Jesus has just reassured his disciples that wherever he is going they will follow, and has promised them 'I am the way, and the truth, and the life; no one comes to the Father, but by me. If you had known me, you would have known my Father also; henceforth you know him and have seen him.' Philip asks, 'Lord, show us the Father, and we shall be satisfied.' Jesus answers, 'Have I been with you so long, and yet you do not know me,

A 19th-century engraving of the Feeding of the Five
Thousand, showing Andrew introducing the boy with his
basket of loaves and fishes to Jesus and his disciples.

Philip? He who has seen me has seen the Father . . . he who loves me will be
loved by my Father, and I will love him and manifest myself to him.'

It seems that Philip was a sincere person, approachable and practical, but
not yet during Jesus's ministry so much a leader as a 'contact man', whose
very simplicity called forth words of Jesus that are still deeply treasured by
Christians: 'He who has seen me has seen the Father.'

The final reference to Nathaniel in the Fourth Gospel relates that after
the Resurrection of Jesus and together with six others, he was fishing in the
Lake of Galilee, when the risen Jesus appeared to them. It may well be that
Philip was one of the two unnamed disciples mentioned in the story. They
had been out all night on the lake and returned at dawn to find Jesus standing
on the beach, though they did not at first recognize him. He called out
to them,

'Children, have you any fish?' They answered him, 'No.' He said to them, 'Cast the net on the right side of the boat, and you will find some.' So they cast it, and now they were not able to haul it in, for the quantity of fish. . . . But the other disciples came in the boat, dragging the net full of fish, for they were not far from the land, but about a hundred yards off. . . . Jesus said to them, 'Come and have breakfast.' Now none of the disciples dared ask him, 'Who are you?' They knew it was the Lord. Jesus came and took the bread and gave it to them, and so with the fish. This was now the third time that Jesus was revealed to the disciples after he was raised from the dead (John 21:5, 6, 8, 12–14).

There is no further reference to either Philip or Nathaniel Bar-Tolmai within the four Gospels. In the Acts, however, the figure of *a* Philip is to be found in three separate chapters (6, 8 and 21), first as one of the seven deacons elected to administer charity in the daily distribution at Jerusalem, and secondly as a successful Christian evangelist in Samaria and Caesarea. He was a man 'of good repute, full of the Spirit and wisdom', selected by the Hellenistic Greek-speaking Jews and commissioned by the apostles with prayer and the laying-on of hands; he supervised the daily distribution of bread to the Hellenist widows and poor in Jerusalem.

The earliest members of the Christian Church in Jerusalem had been mostly pious Jews, who had continued to visit the temple and to observe the Jewish Law. The original disciples of Jesus, perhaps from Galilee or from the neighbourhood of Jerusalem, were Aramaic-speaking. Now, as others, both Jews and foreigners, had come to settle in the city, sometimes residing near the temple, the Christian Church had acquired new members from these newcomers. Christian evangelism had been particularly successful among the Hellenistic Jews, who spoke Greek instead of Aramaic. Consequently there developed in Jerusalem two classes of Christian believers, the Hebrews and the Hellenists, both accepting the Messiahship of Jesus.

The welfare and relief of the needy have always been characteristics of Judaism and the Law insists on providing for the fatherless and the widow, the slave and the stranger. The Christian community gladly accepted such obligations, as may be seen from the very considerable fund for poor relief that Paul brought to Jerusalem from his Mediterranean congregations. There developed, however, a sense of resentment among the Hellenists that their widows were being neglected in the daily distribution at Jerusalem. This threatened to cause some friction between these two groups, the Hebrews and the Hellenists.

The twelve apostles immediately took action, summoning the community as a whole body and ruling, 'It is not right that we should give up preaching the word of God to serve tables. Therefore, brethren, pick out from among you seven men of good repute, full of the Spirit and of wisdom, whom we may appoint to this duty. But we will devote ourselves to prayer and to the ministry of the word' (Acts 6:2–4). The whole Christian community approved this course of action and they chose seven men to undertake the domestic and financial administration of the poor relief. These seven deacons, as they later came to be called, the apostles commissioned by prayer and the laying-on of their hands. Whatever the terms of their commission, certain of them are known to have been involved in teaching and evangelistic work, particularly Stephen and Philip.

The names of the seven – Stephen, Philip, Prochorus, Nicanor, Timon, Parmenas and Nicolaus – all indicate a Greek background, though most of them must have been of Jewish birth.

Following the martyrdom of Stephen and the persecution of Hellenistic Christians, Philip went to Samaria to preach to the people about the Messiah. 'And the multitudes with one accord gave heed to what was said by Philip, when they heard him and saw the signs which he did. For unclean spirits came out of many who were possessed, crying with a loud voice; and many who were paralysed or lame were healed. So there was much joy in that city' (Acts 8:6–8).

Philip the Deacon became a successful evangelist, converting a magician called Simon. 'But when they believed Philip as he preached good news about the kingdom of God and the name of Jesus Christ, they were baptized, both men and women. Even Simon himself believed, and after being baptized he continued with Philip. And seeing signs and great miracles performed, he was amazed' (Acts 8:12–13). Philip's evangelistic efforts were confirmed by a visit from the apostles Peter and John, as a result of which the Christians in Samaria were the first to receive the gift of the Holy Spirit by the 'laying on of hands with prayer'.

Philip is next described as intercepting the chariot of the chief treasurer of the queen of Ethiopia, on his way down from Jerusalem to Gaza. This court official was returning from a pilgrimage to the Holy City and was reading from the prophet Isaiah as he journeyed. Philip asked him if he knew about whom he was reading. The passage was from the Suffering Servant songs of the second Isaiah: 'As a sheep led to the slaughter or a lamb before its shearer is dumb, so he opens not his mouth. In his humiliation justice was denied him. Who can describe his generation? For his life is taken up from the earth' (Acts 8:32, 33). The man turned to Philip and asked, 'About whom, pray, does the prophet say this, about himself or about some one else?' Starting, therefore, with this text of scripture, Philip 'told him the good news of Jesus'. Further along the road the Ethiopian was baptized by Philip at his own request. Later 'Philip was found at Azotus, and passing on he preached the gospel to all the towns till he came to Caesarea' (Acts 8:40). The north African scholar Tertullian, in the beginning of the third century, specifically says that 'Philip *the Apostle* was snatched away from the eunuch', in a commentary on this passage.

It was at Caesarea, in about the year 58, that Paul and Luke were enter-

St Philip baptizing the Ethiopian eunuch on the desert road to Gaza, by Cuyp. The umbrella is a familiar Abyssinian status symbol to this day.

tained by Philip and his four daughters, on Paul's final and fateful journey to Jerusalem. Certainly Philip and Paul had much in common, particularly their purpose in presenting the Gospel of Jesus to the Gentiles. It would seem that Philip was the first missionary to the maritime plain, that it was quite natural that he should settle in the city of Caesarea and that he had already spent twenty years there by the time of Paul's visit.

It has been suggested by recent scholars that the seven 'deacons', although originally chosen for their spiritual qualities to carry out the task of relief provisioning, did in fact become the leaders of the Hellenistic Jewish community. This would account for the rapid rise in importance of Stephen and Philip as evangelists and preachers. Furthermore, the mention of Philip at Caesarea, the administrative capital of the districts of Judaea and Samaria – and seat of the procurator – might well mean that his actual position was equivalent to that of bishop or overseer in the Caesarean Church. It might possibly even strengthen the argument for the identification of this Hellenistic administrator and preacher with the original, and presumably Jewish, fisherman-apostle from Bethsaida, who was the very first to receive the call 'Follow me'.

The New Testament does in fact give clear indications of the characters of Philip and Nathaniel Bar-Tolmai. The somewhat reluctant and pessimistic provisioner of the twelve might well have been confused with the deacon relief-provisioner among the seven. Either man, or possibly the combined single personality, could have become the effective and energetic missionary administrator. Similarly the transparent sincerity, devotion and orthodox scriptural philosophy of Nathaniel Bar-Tolmai, surrendered to the service of the Jewish-Christian Church, was to prove of infinite value and inspiration. If the apocryphal tales of their subsequent travels and trials appear far too legendary and even grotesque to be of any historical value, they follow the trails blazed by two bright comets – Philip across the skies of central Asia, Bartholomew from Armenia to India and back again.

The apocryphal Acts of Philip, probably compiled at the end of the fourth century from older legends, link the two men, Philip and Bartholomew, together. The work relates their mission in Hierapolis, the martyrdom of Philip as both apostle and deacon, and Bartholomew's escape to preach elsewhere. It is a grotesque yet catholic and orthodox novel in fifteen Acts, including the martyrdom. The first Act describes how when Philip had come out of Galilee, a widow was carrying out her only son to burial. She claimed to have spent much money in vain on the gods – Ares, Apollo, Hermes, Artemis, Zeus, Athena, the Sun and Moon – but 'I think they are asleep as far as I am concerned'. Philip raised her son, who was baptized and followed him.

The second Act relates that in Athens Philip met three hundred philosophers who wanted to hear some 'new thing'. Philip claimed the teachings of Jesus as 'new'. The philosophers wrote to the Jewish high priest in Jerusalem, Ananias, who went in person to Athens and explained the story and fate of Jesus to the philosophers, to the effect that he was crucified but that his disciples stole his body. When they assaulted Philip, Ananias and his escort were blinded and the unrepentant Ananias was slowly 'swallowed up by the earth', but his escort was restored and baptized. Philip stayed two years in Athens, founded a Church, ordained a bishop and presbyter, and departed to Parthia to preach. There Philip met both Peter and John, who said: 'Andrew has gone to Achaia and Thrace, Thomas to India and the "wicked flesh-eaters", Matthew to the "savage troglodytes".'

In the days of the Emperor Trajan, following the martyrdom of Simon, son of Clopas, the second bishop in Jerusalem and successor of James the brother of Jesus, Philip was preaching through Lydia and Asia. There, after many travels, miracles and conversions, he met his sister Mariamne and his friend Bartholomew. Together they arrived at Hierapolis, whose people worshipped the great snake or dragon, and there they stayed at the house of a Christian called Stachys. Philip began to preach and the people started to believe the Gospel of Jesus, among them Nicanora, wife of the Roman proconsul. She was apparently a Jewess, who had been cured by Philip of trachoma or some similar disease of the eyes.

The apostles prayed for Nicanora, but

her tyrant husband came and said: 'How is this? Who has healed you?' And she said: 'Depart from me, and lead a chaste and sober life.' And he dragged her by the hair and threatened to kill her. And the apostles were arrested, and scourged and dragged to the temple and shut up in it. The people and the priests came and demanded vengeance on the sorcerors. They stripped and searched the apostles for charms, and pierced Philip's ankles and thighs and hung him head downward, and Bartholomew they hung naked by the hair. And Philip and Bartholomew talked in Hebrew, and Philip said: 'Shall we call down fire from heaven? I shall endure it no longer, let the deep open and swallow these men.' It opened and the whole place was swallowed, about seven thousand men, save where the apostles were. Jesus appeared and rebuked Philip. But he defended himself. And the Lord said: 'Since you have been unforgiving and wrathful, you shall indeed die in glory and be taken by angels to paradise, but shall remain outside it for forty days, in fear of the flaming sword, and then I will send Michael and he shall let you in. And Bartholomew shall go to Lycaonia and be crucified there, and Mariamne's body shall be laid up in the river Jordan. And I shall bring back those who have been swallowed up.' And he drew a cross in the air, reaching down into the abyss, and it was filled with light, and the cross was like a ladder. And Jesus called the people, and they all came up, save the proconsul and the Viper. And seeing the apostles they mourned and repented. and Philip, still hanging, spoke to them and told them of his offence.

'Bury me not in linen like the Lord, but in papyrus, and pray for me forty days. Where my blood is dropping a vine will grow, and ye shall use the wine of it for the cup: and partake of it on the third day.' And he prayed the Lord to receive him, and protect him against all enemies. 'Let not their dark air cover us, that I may pass the waters of fire and all the abyss. Clothe me in thy glorious robe and thy seal of light that ever shineth, until I have passed by all the rulers of the world and the evil dragon that opposeth us.' And he died. And they buried him as he directed. And a heavenly voice said he had received the crown. After three days the vine grew up. And they made the offering daily for forty days, and built the church and made Stachys bishop. And all the city believed. And at the end of forty days the Saviour appeared in the form of Philip and told Bartholomew and Mariamne that he had entered paradise, and bade them go their ways. And Bartholomew went to Lycaonia and Mariamne to Jordan, and Stachys and the brethren abode where they were.

The apocryphal information concerning Bartholomew is rather more varied than that of Philip. There is a Gospel of Bartholomew, mentioned by Jerome at the beginning of the fourth century, which consists of questions put by Bartholomew to Jesus and to his mother Mary before the Ascension.

The opening question is virtually a commentary on the credal clause 'He descended into hell'.

Filippino Lippi's painting of St Philip exorcising the Devil in Hierapolis, where people worshipped 'the Great Dragon', and were responsible for the martyrdom of both Philip and Bartholomew.

But Bartholomew went up to him and said: 'Lord, I wish to speak to you.' Jesus answered him: 'Beloved Bartholomew, I know what you wish to say. Ask then, and I will tell you all you wish to know. And I myself will make known to you what you do not say.' Bartholomew said to him: 'Lord, when you went to be hanged on the cross, I followed you at a distance and saw how you were hanged on the cross and how the angels descended from heaven and worshipped you. And when darkness came, I looked and saw that you had vanished from the cross; only I heard your voice in the underworld, and suddenly there a great wailing and gnashing of teeth arose. Tell me, Lord, where you went from the cross.' And Jesus answered: 'Blessed are you, Bartholomew, my beloved, because you saw this mystery. And now I will tell you everything you ask me. When I vanished from the cross, I went to the underworld to bring up Adam and all the patriarchs, Abraham, Isaac and Jacob. The Archangel Michael had asked me to do this. And I brought out all the patriarchs and came again to the cross.' And Bartholomew said to him: 'Lord, I saw

you again hanging on the cross and all the dead arising and worshipping you. Tell me, Lord, who was he whom the angels carried in their arms, that exceedingly large man? And what did you say to him that he groaned so deeply?' 'It was Adam, the first created, for whose sake I came down from heaven upon the earth. And I said to him: "I was hanged upon the cross for your sake and for the sake of your children." And when he heard that, he groaned and said: "So you were pleased to do, O Lord".'

Similarly the closing question is a commentary on the cardinal sin 'against the Holy Spirit'.

Bartholomew said to him: 'Tell us, Lord, which sin is more grievous than all other sins.' Jesus replied: 'Truly, I say to you that hypocrisy and slander are more grievous than all other sins. Truly, truly, I say to you, that every sin shall be forgiven every man, but the sin against the Holy Spirit shall not be forgiven.' And Bartholomew said: 'What is the sin against the Holy Spirit?' Jesus answered: 'Everyone who decrees against any man who serves my Father has blasphemed against the Holy Spirit. For every man who served God with reverence is worthy of the Holy Spirit, and he who speaks any evil against him shall not be forgiven.'

Towards the end of one of the most inspiring and perceptive of the apocryphal works are these words:

At that time, I, Bartholomew, wrote this in my heart, and I took the hand of the friend of man, and began joyfully to speak thus: Glory be to thee, O Lord Jesus Christ, who givest to all thy grace which we have all perceived. Alleluia. Glory be to thee, O Lord, the life of sinners. Glory be to thee, O Lord, through whom death is put to shame. Glory be to thee, O Lord, the treasure of righteousness. We praise thee as God. Glory be to thee, Holy Father, inextinguishable sun, incomprehensible, full of light. To thee be honour, to thee glory and worship world without end. Amen.

Jerome, who knew and valued this Gospel, had a theory about the origin and ancestry of Bartholomew. He suggested that the apostle might be descended from the Talmai (rather than Tolmai) king of Geshur, mentioned in the Second Book of Samuel (3:3). This Talmai had a daughter who married King David at Hebron and became the mother of Absalom. It is interesting to think of the twelve including one with a royal pedigree, a thousand years old!

There are three separate but not necessarily contradictory traditions about the spheres of Bartholomew's ministry. First that he went to Phrygia with Philip and preached in Hierapolis; secondly that he went to India; thirdly that he was martyred in Armenia. The Indian tradition includes this personal description of Bartholomew:

He has black curly hair, white skin, large eyes, straight nose, his hair covers his ears, his beard long and grizzled, middle height: he wears a white *colobium* with a purple stripe, and a white cloak with four purple 'gems' at the corners: for twenty-six years he has worn these and they never grow old: his shoes have lasted twenty-six years: he prays one hundred times a day and one hundred times a night: his voice is like a trumpet: angels wait upon him: he is always cheerful and knows all languages.

There is some early evidence to confirm the Indian tradition in the works of Eusebius and the scholar Jerome. Eusebius (EH. v. 10) wrote concerning a Christian missionary in the second century:

Pantaenus was constituted a herald of the Gospel of Christ to the nations of the east, and advanced even as far as India. . . . Pantaenus . . . is said to have come to the [land of the] Indians; to have found there that the Gospel according to Matthew had anticipated his own arrival among some who knew Christ and to whom Bartholomew, one of the apostles, had preached and had left them the book of Matthew in Hebrew script, which is also preserved until this time.

In his work on 'Famous Men', Jerome confirmed this record of Eusebius:

Pantaenus . . . was a man of such learning both in Sacred Scriptures and in secular knowledge that he was sent to India by Demetrius, bishop of Alexandria, at the request of that nation's legates. There he found that the coming of Christ, our Lord, according to the Gospel of Matthew, was preached by Bartholomew, one of the twelve apostles.

It would seem that Bartholomew founded a Christian Church in India, whose messengers in later years were sent as far as Alexandria in order to invite Christian teachers. A fifth-century Hieronymian martyrology refers to the feast day: 'On the 9th Kalends of September the natal day of St Bartholomew the Apostle who was beheaded for Christ in Citerior India, by order of King Astriagis.' 'Citerior India' implies 'near India' or the north-west coast. This is confirmed by a tenth-century Byzantine tradition that 'the Apostle Bartholomew went to India *Felix*, or Happy', which is a translation of the Sanskrit word *Kalyana*, the name of a city in the neighbourhood of Bombay. The eighth-century martyrology of the Venerable Bede has the following entry: 'The Natal Day of St Bartholomew the Apostle who, preaching the Gospel of Christ in India, was flayed alive and being beheaded by order of King Astriagis completed martyrdom.'

The third tradition is that Bartholomew was martyred in Armenia, at Albanopolis – the modern Derbend – south of the Caucasus. This has been the claim of the Armenian Church, who have revered Bartholomew as their founder for nearly fourteen hundred years.

The early seventh-century historical geographer, Isidore of Seville, says 'Bartholomew the Apostle . . . translated the Gospel of Matthew among the Indians into their own language. Finally he was flayed alive by cruel and barbarous people in Albano, a city of Major Armenia; and so he is buried there.' Another seventh-century writer, known as Pseudo-Sophronius, writes 'the Apostle Bartholomew preached the Gospel of Christ to the Indians who are called the Happy, and entrusted them with the Gospel according to Matthew. He, however, fell asleep in Albanopolis, a city of Major Armenia'.

A ninth-century martyrologist refers to 'The Natal Day of Bartholomew the Apostle who preached in Lycaonia . . . in the end was flayed alive by barbarians in Albano a city of Major Armenia; and by order of King Astriagis he was beheaded and thus buried on the 24th of August.' And the Armenian called Pseudo-Moses of Chorene, in the eighth century claimed: 'There came then into Armenia the Apostle Bartholomew, who suffered martyrdom among us in the town of Arepan.'

The only 'Passion' describing the martyrdom of Bartholomew in any detail may be traced to the end of the sixth century, though it may draw some material from the fourth-century apocryphal Acts of John. There is a single Greek manuscript dated 1279, though the Latin manuscripts go back to the eighth or ninth centuries. It is from this work that the personal description

of Bartholomew, already quoted, comes. The narrative of his martyrdom immediately follows that portrait.

For two days they could not find him, but then he cast a devil out of a man. King Polymius heard of it and sent for him to heal his lunatic daughter who bit every one. She was loosed – the apostle having reassured her keepers – and cured. The king sent camels laden with riches, but the apostle could not be found. Next day, however, he came to the king and expounded the Christian faith, and offered to show him the devil who had inhabited his idol. There was a dialogue, in which the demon explained his doings. Bartholomew made the people try to pull the statue down, but they could not. The ropes were removed, and he bade the demon leave the statue, which was instantly broken. After a prayer of the apostle, an angel appeared and signed the four corners of the temple with a cross; and then showed them the devil: black, sharp-faced, with long beard, hair to the feet, fiery eyes, breathing flame, spiky wings like a hedgehog, bound with fiery chains; and then the angel sent him away howling. The king and the rest were baptized. But the heathen priests went and complained to his brother Astriges [Astyages], who had Bartholomew bound, and questioned him. It was told him that his idol Vualdath had fallen and was broken to pieces, and in anger he had Bartholomew beaten with clubs and beheaded [the Greek puts in 'flayed', in accordance with the late tradition]. And the people buried him honourably, and built a basilica over him. After twenty days Astriges was seized by a devil, and he and all the priests died. And there was great fear, and all believed: the king [Polymius] became bishop and presided twenty years.

OPPOSITE ABOVE The Flaying of Bartholomew, traditionally in Albano, Armenia, at the order of King Astriagis – a mosaic in St Mark's, Venice.

OPPOSITE BELOW Another mosaic from St Mark's shows St Philip directing the pulling down of an idol and exorcising a devil.

6 Matthew and James, Sons of Alphaeus

In all four lists of apostles, within the Synoptic Gospels and the Acts, occur the names of Matthew and of James, the son of Alphaeus. Matthew is listed seventh or eighth, and James always in the ninth place. The Gospel according to Matthew specifies that Matthew was a tax-collector. A fourth-century commentary by the great bishop and scholar, John Chrysostom of Constantinople, shows that there was a strong early tradition that *both* Matthew and James were tax-collectors.

There is no account in the Gospels of the call of James, the son of Alphaeus. The call of Matthew is related in all the Synoptic Gospels, but in Mark and Luke he is referred to as '*Levi*, the son of Alphaeus'. Assuming the priority of the Marcan version, Matthew and Luke follow Mark *verbatim*, except that Matthew changes the name of 'Levi' to 'Matthew'. When, however, the three synoptists list the twelve apostles, all three omit the name of 'Levi' in favour of the name of 'Matthew'. Furthermore, in the list of apostles present at Pentecost, there is again no mention of Levi, but only of Matthew. Therefore, it is sound to assume that Levi became known as Matthew (meaning the gift of God). The two names refer to one and the same tax-collector, called by Jesus from his desk at the frontier town of Capernaum.

The references to 'Levi' show too that Matthew was another 'son of Alphaeus' and that Matthew and James were probably brother publicans. 'Publicans' were so called in the King James Version from the Latin *publicani*, referring to those employed in collecting the public revenue.

In the story of the Crucifixion of Jesus, Mark and Matthew tell of the women 'looking on from afar'. They say that the women were Mary Magdalene, Salome the mother of the sons of Zebedee, and also Mary, the mother of James 'the Younger' and Joses. This last Mary is also mentioned in the Crucifixion account in the Fourth Gospel, as 'Mary, the wife of Clopas'. She appears again with the women who went to anoint the body of Jesus early on the Easter morning, but here she is called 'Mary, the mother of James' (Mark 16:1).

The sons of Alphaeus and their symbols: St Matthew and his angel (above), St James and the club with which he was martyred; by Luca Della Robbia, Church of the Holy Cross, Florence.

If this 'James the Younger, son of Clopas' was the same as 'James, son of Alphaeus', there must be an identification of the two fathers' names. And in fact there is. The Hebrew *Halphai*, within the Talmud Kiddushin (58b) and the Aramaic *Chalpai*, in the First Book of Maccabees (11:70) are almost transliterated into *Clopas*. This in the Greek form becomes *Alphios*, for the Greeks, like the English, drop their aitches. The Latin poet Horace writes of a Jewish moneylender called Alphius. The same consonants survive in the Arabic root *Halafa*, meaning 'friend' or 'ally'. Thus, James's father appears under three different names within the Gospels: Alphaeus, Clopas and Cleopas, the disciple who met the risen Jesus on the road to Emmaus. The son James is mentioned seven times in the New Testament.

Hegesippus, a second-century Church historian and native of Palestine whose Memoirs have been partly preserved within the *Ecclesiastical History* of Eusebius, said that Clopas was the brother of Joseph the carpenter of Nazareth. This would make Alphaeus/Clopas/Cleopas an uncle of Jesus of Nazareth and the two apostles Matthew and James 'the Younger' (together with their brother Joseph) first cousins of Jesus. Matthew and James would also be distantly related to James and John, the sons of Zebedee, also first cousins of Jesus, but on his mother's side.

The actual scriptural information about the brothers Matthew and James is negligible; not a word or opinion survives within the Gospels. Although very little is known personally about them, a great deal may be inferred from their occupation.

Tax-gatherers were likely to be prosperous, and were certain to be regarded with particular loathing for co-operating with the occupying power for their own financial gain. They were particularly likely to be despised within a Jewish community, as sinners and outside the Law. Matthew's Gospel describes Jesus himself classing tax-collectors with Gentiles and harlots, as the lowest of the low, in his condemnation of certain Scribes and Pharisees. 'Truly I say to you, the tax-collectors and the harlots go into the Kingdom of God before you.' The Jews, however, grouped tax-collectors with murderers and robbers, excluding them from giving judgement or even evidence in court and excommunicating them from public worship, hence 'the tax-collector, standing far off' in the temple, in the parable of the Pharisee and the publican.

During the republic, the Roman state relieved itself of the trouble and expense of collecting the taxes of the provinces by putting them up for auction among the great Roman financial corporations, one of whom would buy for a fixed sum the right to collect within each province. The members of the company, usually from the equestrian order, would make the best they could out of the bargain, and squeeze all possible profit from the transaction. The corporations employed highly skilled staffs, who could be seconded to any province to organize the business of collection. Results were often dependent upon the integrity or corruption of the provincial governor concerned; on one occasion the provincials of Asia were forced to pay their taxes three times over.

One example is the tax-collector, Joseph, in the second century BC, from the village of Phicola, who established himself at Jerusalem. From there he directed the collection of taxes from Syria, Phoenicia, Judaea and Samaria and held the position for twenty-two years. He had an office in Alexandria from which his steward made payments into the royal Treasury. Such men established themselves as bankers and wholesale traders at Jerusalem, and mortgaged the land and crops of the peasants (Josephus Ant. 12:175).

Under the imperial system, state machinery for collecting taxes replaced the private enterprise of the financial corporations. In each province, a procurator appointed by the emperor supervised the collection of revenue, using local agents who were often natives of the province. These men were regarded as 'quislings' who had sold themselves into the service of the occupying forces for their private profit.

There were two distinct kinds of taxes: statutory taxes and customs dues. The statutory rates were well known and allowed little possibility for abuse. They included a ground tax of one-tenth of the grain crop and one-fifth of the wine crop, an income tax of one per cent of annual income, and a poll tax (for men over fourteen and women over twelve) of one denarius, the equivalent of a day's pay in each year.

As there were two kinds of taxes, there were two sorts of tax-collectors. Customs dues were the subject of endless levies, necessitating innumerable collectors, usually one for each category of duty in each township or district. The main source of government revenue was the export and import dues, the tariff varying from 2·5 to 12·5 per cent on the value of the goods. There was also a purchase tax on all articles bought and sold, and many trade licences and market dues on the mass of local produce brought to market every day of the week. There were the town dues on all citizens and travellers entering walled towns. There were also many travel tolls: road tolls, bridge tolls, river-crossing tolls, harbour and quay tolls.

The *Pax Romana* was a costly luxury demanding a vast revenue from a multiplicity of taxes gathered by a multitude of civil servants. Customs men had a warrant to stop, to search and to strip, to examine goods and impose such dues as they thought fit. Customs officers could demand military escort and enforcement. In Judaea and Samaria, taxation was administered by the imperial procurator of Judaea, in Galilee by Herod Antipas as a vassal responsible to Rome. From AD 6 to 66, the burden of taxation in Judaea remained constant at 600 talents (Josephus Ant. 17:320), although in AD 17 the provinces of Judaea and Samaria begged for a reduction, without success. Herod Antipas in Galilee, however, inherited his father's progressive and insatiable ambition, also his costly and lavish display, which had to

The calling of St Matthew from his customs desk at Capernaum, by
Clement O. Skilbeck.

be met from the public revenues.

Matthew and James seem to have been customs officers rather than statutory tax-collectors. Matthew's call took place at Capernaum, after Jesus had healed a paralysed man in Simon Peter's house. Capernaum was a frontier town almost in the centre of the north shore of the lake, astride the road from Damascus to the Mediterranean port of Acre. The mouth of the Jordan where it flowed into the lake formed the frontier, crossed by the road as it left the territory of Herod Philip, tetrarch of Iturea, Gaulanitis and Trachonitis, and as it entered the territory of Herod Antipas, tetrarch of Galilee and Perea. With traffic both on the road and on the lake, the customs office must have been very much at the centre of the post. The two brothers were likely therefore to have both seen and heard Jesus passing by. Consequently, when Jesus actually called Matthew, he was 'ready' to follow and even to entertain Jesus together with his fellow publicans. However unlikely a choice, he at once got up to follow Jesus.

Matthew describes his call thus: 'Getting into a boat he crossed over and came to his own city . . . as Jesus passed on from there, he saw a man called Matthew sitting at the tax office; and he said to him, "Follow me." And he rose and followed him' (Matt. 9:1 and 9). Luke goes on to describe what followed: 'And Levi made him a great feast in his house; and there was a large company of tax collectors and others sitting at table with them. And the Pharisees and their scribes murmured against his disciples, saying, "Why do you eat and drink with tax collectors and sinners?" And Jesus answered them, "Those who are well have no need of a physician, but those who are sick; I have not come to call the righteous, but sinners to repentance."' (Luke 5:29–32). Luke clearly points out that the guest of honour at this party was Jesus and that it was held at Matthew's own house. Indeed, he must have been a man of some substance to be able to entertain such a company of his own cronies within his own house. Might not his publican brother James have acted as a brother host on this occasion?

The frontier town of Capernaum, destined to become the headquarters of the Galilean mission of Jesus and the twelve, had a busy harbour, with boats from neighbouring ports loading and off-loading the dried fish and local wares of Galilee, the silks and spices of Damascus, the fruit and produce of Gennesaret.

Of all the towns in Israel, none was more appropriate for Jesus to launch his message and ministry than the little metropolis of Capernaum. It was the commercial centre of a chain of fishing towns and villages, from Magdala on the west to Gergasa on the east, whose inhabitants brought their daily catch to the wharves and salteries of their market town. Half a mile of lakeside ruins and a considerable depth of water witness to the harbour and warehouse installations of long ago. An infinite variety of local produce must have changed hands here: wool and cloth from Magdala, pigeons bred for the sacrificial purposes of the temple in Jerusalem (hence the Gulf of Pigeons), figs, pomegranates, grapes, dates and almonds from Gennesaret, besides all manner of fish from the lake. The town was in fact one vast sea-bound market place, a cosmopolis, teaming with merchants from Phoenicia and Damascus, Greeks from the Ten Towns and wholesale buyers from Jerusalem.

Less conspicuous, perhaps, within the jostling crowds along the jetties, were the stevedores and shipwrights, the local fisher-folk, both men and women, unloading, sorting, pickling and packing; others mending nets, painting boats and sail-making. Along the coastal highway and the roads leading down to the harbour rolled the ox-carts heaped high with vegetables and fruit, to the accompaniment of the bells of the long trains of camels, roped nose to tail, plodding through the dust or standing, bored yet patient, under vast loads in the thick of the traffic jam. On all sides moved the

From the beach at Capernaum, looking west along the north coast of Galilee, over the Plain of Gennesaret to the Valley of Pigeons.

A 20th-century reconstruction of a 3rd-century synagogue which includes masonry and ornamentation from its 1st-century predecessor, complete with Gentile courtyard and women's gallery.

ubiquitous donkeys and mules, to the shouts and blows of their owners. Every now and then, among the crush, appeared the plumed helmet of a Roman legionary, the black gown of a rabbi, Pharisee or scribe, and the brass badge of a publican – each with his own particular business among the mêlée of men and animals.

The site of Capernaum today, which fits in well with the Gospel references and has been the resort of Christian pilgrims since the fourth century, is that of Kefar Nahum – the village of Nahum – standing on a site called Tell-Hum, where a Byzantine church was discovered in 1921. There is no mound or tell, however, and the name Tell-Hum may well be a corruption of the name of a Jewish rabbi called Tanhum buried in this place and mentioned in the Talmud. It has more recently been suggested that Tell-Hum may be a corruption of the Greek word for 'customs house', *telonion*, which links up with the call of the disciple, Matthew, from the 'receipt of custom'. Certainly, the town lay on the main road to Damascus, within a few kilometres of the Jordan river frontier.

Both Matthew and Luke describe an event at Capernaum, the healing of the centurion's servant, a story which links up with the reconstruction of a very early synagogue to be seen in Capernaum today. The centurion sent a message to Jesus begging his help. Luke says that the centurion had a servant – presumably the equivalent of a batman – who was desperately ill. Matthew adds that he was paralysed and in great pain. In Luke's account the centurion himself never appears, but the Jewish elders commend him and his request to Jesus. The centurion's friends then bring the message that he is not worthy to receive Jesus into his house: 'Lord, do not trouble yourself. . . . But say the word, and let my servant be healed,' runs the message. Jesus then says to the crowd following him, 'I tell you, not even in Israel have I found such faith.' And when the messengers get back to the house they find the servant in perfect health.

This centurion was possibly one of the Gentiles who attended worship at the Jewish synagogue, a 'God-fearer', as Paul called them. Luke describes how the elders reported that 'he loves our nation, and he built us our synagogue'. Today, at Capernaum, is to be seen a third-century reconstruction into which are incorporated *both* Roman *and* Jewish designs. This synagogue has been partially restored; it was well built of white limestone, contrasting vividly with the black lava of the surrounding houses. The prayer hall was rectangular, nearly eighty feet long and fifty-three feet wide. To the east of the prayer hall was an open courtyard, entered by two doors on the south side. Both hall and courtyard were colonnaded, the columns in the hall supporting the gallery, those in the courtyard forming a cloister facing a doorway into the hall. Through this doorway the Gentile 'God-fearers' might listen to the synagogue service.

The whole building was elaborately decorated with carved stone ornaments. Its walls may have been covered with frescoes, like those of the almost contemporary Dura synagogue, built in AD 244. As Professor Albright has pointed out, the catacombs in Rome and the necropolis at Beth She'arim demonstrate the dependence of early Christian art on Jewish frescoes of the Roman period. What is really striking at Capernaum is the variety of the motifs, particularly the mixture of Jewish and Roman symbols. Among the former are the *menorah* (the seven-branched candlestick), the *shofar* (the ram's horn), the *magen David* (the shield of David), the Ark of the Covenant, the manna pot, and that old symbol of the land, the palm tree.

Among the Roman symbols, two have particular significance for the Christian. The first is the regimental crest of the Tenth Legion, two eagles back to back and beak to beak. The second is the Roman army's equivalent of the Victoria Cross: it was awarded to a soldier who saved the life of an officer in battle. It is a victor's laurel-wreath tied in a circle with a reef-knot

Among the mixture of motifs from the 1st-century synagogue are the Manna Pot (right), reminiscent of the provisioning of the Israelites during their forty years in the desert, and, surprisingly, the regimental crest of the Tenth Legion, eagles holding the laurel wreath of victory.

and enclosing a round sea-shell. The eagles in the regimental crest are holding the same laurel-wreath in their beaks. What is the explanation of this combination of symbols?

Although this is a late second-century or early third-century building, Professor Albright is certain that it stands on the site of an earlier synagogue. This latter may possibly have been that in which Jesus worshipped, taught and healed. It may well be that carvings of this synagogue were moved on to the later building. Coupled with the story in Luke's Gospel, this could explain how the regimental crest of a Roman legion came to adorn the very keystone of a Jewish synagogue (Luke 7:1–10).

Certainly the synagogue at Capernaum – even in the first century – was of noble proportions compared with the living-quarters whose basalt ruins have been excavated nearby. Among these is an octagonal Byzantine shrine, which the Franciscans claim marks the site of the house of Peter's mother-in-law. It is this house that became the base of operations for the twelve in Galilee. One might like to think of it as a fisherman's cottage at the water's edge, with a dinghy on the strand and nets out to dry, though Mark indicates that the house was near the synagogue in the centre of the town. 'And immediately he left the synagogue, and entered the house of Simon and Andrew, with James and John' (Mark 1:29).

Matthew refers to Capernaum as Jesus's 'own city' (9:1). Mark says, 'When he returned to Capernaum after some days, it was reported that he was at home' (2:1). However much Jesus may have felt at home there, Capernaum – like Jerusalem – rejected him and remained for three centuries a Jewish settlement. It is not surprising that so many of the twelve had direct associations with Capernaum. The very centre of the whole Galilean fishing industry became their natural headquarters and meeting place. But amid the limestone and basalt ruins that once hummed and buzzed with the thriving activity of the frontier town and port, these words recorded by Matthew still echo down the years, as they echoed once across the lake. 'And you, Capernaum, will you be exalted to heaven? You shall be brought down to Hades. For if the mighty works done in you had been done in Sodom, it would have remained until this day' (Matt. 11:23–24).

So much may be deduced from the occupation and environment of the two brothers. About James the Younger, little more is known and legend records that his mission was to Persia, where he died by crucifixion. The chief source of information about Matthew, however, is the Gospel unanimously attributed to him by the early Church Fathers. It is surprising to find that the writer of this Gospel follows so closely the narrative of Mark's Gospel rather than presenting his own record of events; but this may perhaps be explained by his concentration upon the teaching rather than the life of Jesus as his own particular contribution.

According to Papias (c. 60–130), bishop of Hierapolis in Asia Minor,

Matthew made a collection of the sayings of Jesus in Hebrew. Eusebius quotes the Alexandrian biblical scholar Origen as saying that 'Matthew, who had preached earlier to the Hebrews, when he was about to go to others also, committed his Gospel in writing in his own tongue' (i.e. Aramaic rather than Hebrew).

Whether this is the Gospel to be found in the New Testament it is not possible to say with certainty. The Gospel according to Matthew is in part a manual of Christian teaching, in which Jesus the Messiah is shown to be both the fulfilment of God's purpose revealed in the Hebrew Scriptures and the Lord of the Christian Church in the New Testament. It is an account of the ministry of Jesus from the pen of a rabbi, completed in the last quarter of the first century. It was traditionally held to be the oldest of the four Gospels, and consequently is placed first in the New Testament. From the beginning of the fourth century it was consistently attributed to Matthew. But its contents seem to show it to be the work neither of an apostle nor of an eye-witness. The narrative of the life of Jesus in it is based on the Gospel of Mark, into which has been inserted much material, mostly about the teaching of Jesus, in five long discourses. For example, chapters 3 and 4, being narrative largely from Mark, are followed by chapters 5, 6 and 7 of the 'long discourse' or the Sermon on the Mount. Chapter 8 and part of 9, taken from Mark, are followed by more chapters of teaching.

The Gospel is a skilfully compiled and comprehensive work, combining at least two other written documents, of which one, containing an account of the teaching of Jesus, may be the record made by Matthew himself, and the reason behind the attribution of the whole Gospel to him. Matthew's training in accountancy and record-keeping may well have been very useful to Jesus and the twelve. In this Gospel, the teaching of Jesus is carefully collected, divided according to subjects, and inserted at appropriate points in Mark's narrative. Almost all of Mark's Gospel is included in that of Matthew. The incidents recorded by Mark are sometimes shortened in Matthew, with some loss of vividness and graphic description. Matthew consciously adjusts Mark's bluntness, for the sake of reverence and propriety, on many occasions. For example, in this Gospel it is the disciples and not Jesus who forget to take food when they cross over the lake. Jesus did no miracles in Nazareth, according to Matthew, because of the people's lack of faith. Mark had written 'He could do no mighty work there'. Matthew does not include the terrified cry of the disciples to Jesus in the storm on the lake: 'Do you not care if we perish?'

This Gospel has certain specific points of interest with regard to the character of Jesus as the Messiah, the teacher, and the law-giver of the Church. It was written after the controversy within the early Christian Church about the admission of Gentile Christians, resolved in the year 42 by the first Council of Jerusalem. Before that time, the Judeo-Christian Church

The instruments and regulations for circumcision.

was divided into two parties, clashing over their attitudes to the observance by the Gentiles of the Law of Moses. A 'circumcision' party held that all Christians must keep the Jewish Law and be circumcised. The other party among the Judeo-Christians considered the Law of Christ sufficient for the Gentiles. The Gospel-writers seem to reflect this division of opinion in their presentation of the Law of Moses as taught by the Pharisees, and of its interpretation and fulfilment by Jesus.

The writer of the First Gospel sought to prove that Christianity was the fulfilment of Judaism, and that Jesus's mission was primarily to the Jews, whose failure to respond to it had been followed by its extension to the Gentiles. He sought to show the teaching of Jesus to be the new Law, and the Christian Church of Jews and Gentiles to be the new Israel. There is a recurring emphasis on the fulfilment of the Old Testament in the person of Jesus, the 'son of David'. Mark often alluded to the Old Testament prophecies; Matthew used them independently of their original context in what may seem to be a somewhat artificial fashion, showing their fulfilment in Jesus. Perhaps these Messianic 'proof-texts' were part of a collection in circulation within the early Church and this collection was the work of Matthew himself, mentioned by Papias in the second century.

Unlike Mark, Matthew does not say that the Messiahship of Jesus was hidden. The voice at his baptism proclaims to all, 'This is my beloved Son.' The disciples, seeing Jesus walking on the water, declare 'Truly you are the Son of God', long before Peter confesses, 'You are the Christ'. Matthew adds to the story of Peter's confession given in Mark, the words spoken by Jesus, 'And on this rock I will build my church,' implying that the secret of Jesus's identity and of his victory through suffering is to be enshrined in the community of his followers, the Church.

The great contribution of Matthew to the total picture of Jesus in the Gospels is his careful record of the teaching of Jesus about the principles upon which life is to be lived under the rule of God. The teaching of Jesus about these principles is carefully grouped into five discourses – a sort of Christian Pentateuch – as follows: the Sermon on the Mount (chapters 5, 6 and 7); the Instructions to the Apostles (chapter 10: 5–42); a Collection of Parables (chapter 13: 1–52); Relationships within the Church (chapter 18: 1–35); the Discourse on the End of the World (chapters 24 and 25). This account of the teaching of Jesus Christ was a source of guidance to the early Church; it can still be read as one continuous instruction, set within the story of the life, death and Resurrection of Jesus.

The Sermon on the Mount, as presented in Matthew's Gospel, has won universal homage as a supreme statement of the ethical duties of man. It is a statement of the Christian standard of life, but makes a general appeal to the human conscience of all men. It does not, at first sight, seem to vary from what is best in the ethics of Confucius, of the Buddha, or indeed of the

Pharisees of Jesus's own day. The Sermon is not so much a detailed state-ment of principles as a series of illustrations of the way in which those principles work in actual living. The principles are twofold.

The first is self-renunciation: 'If any man would come after me, let him deny himself and take up his cross and follow me. For whoever would save his life will lose it, and whoever loses his life for my sake will find it.' The second is service: 'Whoever would be great among you must be your servant, and whoever would be first among you must be your slave.' Jesus offers himself as the supreme illustration: 'The Son of Man came not to be served but to serve, and to give his life as a ransom for many.'

The Sermon on the Mount begins with a list of spiritual qualities and the rewards that accompany them: 'Blessed are the poor in spirit, for theirs is the kingdom of heaven.' The task of the disciples in the world is illustrated by the metaphors of salt and light. Their true piety can be seen in *secret* giving, praying and fasting. Their trust in God's providence is to be that of the birds and the flowers. They are to go on asking from God, who loves to give to those who ask him. They are not to criticize, like a man with a log in his own eye seeing a splinter in that of his neighbour.

The 'golden rule' is given: 'Whatever you wish that men would do to you, do so to them; for this is the law and the prophets.' And the Sermon ends with a terrifyingly simple story of the man who builds his house on the rock of obedience and action, contrasted with the man who builds his house on the sands of apathy and inaction. 'And when Jesus finished these sayings, the crowds were astonished at his teaching, for he taught them as one who had authority, and not as their scribes.' As Moses on Mount Sinai gave the Ten Commandments, so Jesus on the mountain in Galilee gave the new Law, not commandments so much as ideals. The existence of the Law of Moses made the tradition of the Scribes necessary, for it was only by a traditional interpretation of the Law that it could be applied to any particular day and circumstance. For instance, if keeping the Sabbath involved not working, it was necessary for tradition to define what constituted work in that day and age.

For Jesus, the Law was to be obeyed by willing assent to principles. For a system of written law, he substituted a law of the heart. 'You have heard that it was said, "You shall not commit adultery." But I say to you that every one who looks at a woman lustfully has already committed adultery with her in his heart.' The old Law sought to cure the disease of sin by treating its symptoms as seen in the outward action. Jesus tried rather to prevent sin at the stage of intention, and to deal with evil in the heart before it reached the hand.

The ethical teaching of Jesus in the Sermon on the Mount is unique. Matthew's careful record and selection is invaluable, not only to the Christian but to all people of faith and for all time. As Matthew, at the

The modern basilica, on the Mount of Beatitudes overlooking the north shore of the Lake, and here looking southwards to the exit of the River Jordan.

beginning of his Gospel, tells the story of the wise men from the east coming to the newly born king and saviour, so he ends with Jesus's commission to his apostles to 'Go therefore and make disciples of all nations'.

Besides the canonical Gospel of Matthew, there are at least two apocryphal Gospels attributed to him. Jerome says that:

Matthew in Judaea was the first to compose the Gospel of Christ in the Hebrew character and speech for the sake of those who came over to the faith from Judaism; who he was who later translated it into Greek is no longer known with certainty. Further the Hebrew text itself is still preserved in the library at Caesarea which the martyr Pamphilus collected with great care. The Nazaraeans in Beroea, a city of Syria, who use this book, also permitted me to copy it.

It is unlikely that Jerome saw the Hebrew original of Matthew's Gospel in the library at Caesarea, for Eusebius never mentions that such an important document was there. It is more likely that this was the Aramaic manuscript known as the Gospel of the Nazaraeans (Nazarenes), written in the first half of the second century. Only fragments remain today, but in content and compass this Gospel was very closely related to the Gospel of Matthew.

Its Nativity narrative has been lost, but the Temptations, the Sermon on the Mount, healings and discourses survive, together with some of the parables, including that of the Talents. The Passion narrative includes Peter's denial, the release of Barabbas, the miracles at the Crucifixion and the watchmen stupified at the Resurrection.

Another second-century apocryphal Gospel of Ebionites was in fact a heretical adaptation of Matthew's Gospel by a Jewish Christian sect, which denied the virgin birth and the double nature of Jesus as both God and man.

Eusebius, in his *Ecclesiastical History* (V. 10:3), tells of an early tradition according to which Pantaenus, a Christian missionary to India, came upon Christian churches; their founder, St Bartholomew, had brought with him a Hebrew Gospel of St Matthew. St Augustine of Hippo declared that only 'Matthew wrote a Gospel in Hebrew, while the others wrote in Greek'. Subsequent tradition and legend about Matthew is fantastic and contradictory, but there is general agreement that his ministry began among his own countrymen in Hebrew.

Thereafter, there is an infinite variety of opinion: Eusebius says he went to Ethiopia, Ambrose to Persia, Paulinus of Nola to Parthia, Isidore to Macedonia. Clement of Alexandria credits Matthew with a natural death and the Jewish Talmud gives a rather later account of his condemnation and death at the hands of the Sanhedrin. Unfortunately there is some confusion between a sixth-century Acts of Andrew and Matthias, and a somewhat later Acts of Matthew, which appears in places to follow the earlier work. The surviving fragments of both these two Acts relate a martyrdom in a far-off land of cannibals, after a series of hair-raising adventures, in which

Andrew is the companion of both Matthias and Matthew. This would seem to indicate that the Acts of Matthew, being the later work, is perhaps a perversion of the Acts of Andrew and Matthias.

The martyrdom of Matthew, within the Acts of Matthew, begins with a vision in which the apostle is commanded to return to the scene of his former mission.

'Now take my staff and go to Myrna the city of the man-eaters, and plant it at the gate of the church which you and Andrew founded. It will become a tree, and a spring will rise at its foot, and the man-eaters will eat of the tree and wash in the spring, and their bodies will be changed and they will be ashamed of their nakedness, and use fire to cook their food, and learn to know me.'

At the city gate he was met by Phulbana the king's wife, Phulbanos his son and Erba his wife, all possessed by devils – and the devils cried out and threatened Matthew that they would rouse the king against him. He cast them out. The bishop Plato heard and came out to meet him with the clergy. And Matthew preached to the people, and planted the staff. And the people became humanized. He baptized the queen and the rest. At dawn the staff was become a tree. Phulbanus the king was pleased with all this at first, but when they refused to quit Matthew he resolved to burn him.

Matthew had a consoling vision, and warned the people of his death. The devil whom he had cast out disguised himself as a soldier and went to the king, and advised him to seize Matthew. He sent four soldiers, who could only hear two men talking [Matthew and Plato], and then ten, who were routed by seeing a child with a torch. The devil described to the king the difficulty of seizing Matthew, and all that he could do. The king said: 'Take him yourself.' 'I cannot, for he has destroyed all our race.' 'Who, then, are you?' said the king. 'I am the demon Asmodaeus who was in your wife.'

That day the king remained quiet, but next day took two soldiers and went to the church and sent for Matthew. He came out with Plato, but the king could not see him. Matthew opened his eyes. The king treacherously led him to the palace. They pinned him hand and foot to the earth and covered him with papyrus soaked in dolphin oil, and poured brimstone, asphalt and pitch on him, and heaped up tow and wood. And the fire turned to dew, and all the people praised God. Much charcoal from the royal baths was brought, and the twelve gods of gold and silver were set round the fire.

The fire blazed up, and the king said: 'Where is now your magic?' But all the fire flew out about the idols and melted them – whose weight was 1,000 talents of gold. And the king lamented that gods of stone and clay were superior. The fire burnt up many soldiers, and then took the form of a dragon and chased the king to the palace, and curled round so that he could not go in and made him come back to Matthew, crying for help. Matthew rebuked the fire with prayer, and gave up the ghost.

The king had him borne in state to the palace. The body and robes were intact, and sometimes he was seen on the bier, sometimes following or preceding it, and laying his hand on Plato's head. And many sick were healed. When they reached the

An early 16th-century mural of St Matthew with the angel, from the School of
Ghirlandaio, now in the Church of Sancta Maria Novello, at Florence.

palace Matthew was seen to rise from the bier and ascend to heaven, led by a
beautiful child, and twelve men in crowns, and we saw the child crown him. The
king had a coffin made of iron and sealed it with lead, and privately put it on a ship
at midnight and sank it in the sea.

All night the brethren watched at the palace gate, and at dawn a voice came:
'Plato, take the Gospel and the psalter and go to the east of the palace and sing
Alleluia, and read the gospel, and offer of the bread and the vine, pressing three
clusters into the cup, and communicate with me, as the Lord Jesus showed us the
offering that is above, on the third day after he rose.' So it was done, and the chanter
went up on a great stone and sang: 'Precious in the sight of the Lord . . . I slept and
rose up again. . . . And they answered: Shall not the sleeper awake? . . . Now will I
arise, saith the Lord. Alleluia.' They read the gospel and made the offering.

It was about the sixth hour, and Plato looked out to sea seven stadia away, and
lo, Matthew standing on the sea between two men in bright apparel, and the
beautiful child before them. And they said, 'Amen, Alleluia.' And the sea was to

look upon like a crystal stone, and before the Child a cross came up out of the deep, and at the lower end of it the coffin of Matthew: and in a moment it was set on the land where they were.

The king beheld all from a window, and came down and fell at their feet and confessed his sin and his belief. He would give them the palace for a sanctuary, and the coffin should be laid on his golden couch in the great hall. Plato baptized and communicated him.

The apostle appeared and renamed the king with his own name 'Matthew' and gave Christian names to the rest of his family. He then ordained the king a priest, being thirty-seven years, his son a deacon, being seventeen years: his wife a priestess [presbytis] and his son's wife a deaconess, being seventeen years.

The king destroyed his idols, and issued a decree establishing the new faith. Matthew bade them offer the offering daily for forty-nine days and repeat it yearly, and told Plato he should join him in three years, and be succeeded by the king, and he by his son. Then with two angels he departed to heaven.

Beneath the phantasy of such legends may lie a vein of truth that at least one of the brothers died for his faith in a country far from his native Israel.

7 Simon the Zealot and Judas, Son of James

In all the lists of the apostles within the New Testament the tenth and eleventh names are Simon 'the Cananaean' or 'the Zealot' and Judas, son of James, called by Mark and Matthew 'Thaddaeus' and further indicated in the Fourth Gospel by the addition of 'not Iscariot'. There is a problem of identification of these two apostles, Simon and Judas.

Simon is listed by Luke in both his Gospel and the Acts in the tenth place and called 'the Zealot', a term which may apply to his own temperament or perhaps to his political party. He is listed within the Marcan tradition, followed by Matthew, in the eleventh place and called 'the Cananaean'. This word 'Cananaean' is Aramaic for 'the zealous one'; it is not connected with Canaan, though some would say it might refer to a resident of the village of Cana in Galilee. It is more likely, however, that the term *kananaios* applied to Simon in the more ancient manuscripts is derived from the Hebrew verb *kani* meaning 'to be jealous' and is commonly used for someone 'jealous for the Law'. The exact equivalent of *kana* in Greek is *zelotes*, the term used by the Greek-speaking Luke, and translated in the *Revised Standard Version* as 'the Zealot'. Therefore, in all four lists of apostles, the implication may well be that this Simon was a member of the Zealot party.

'Judas, son of James', is so listed by Luke in both his volumes in the eleventh place, while the Marcan tradition places him tenth and calls him 'Thaddaeus' – except in the Western text where 'Lebbaeus' replaces 'Thaddaeus'. Both these names could come from Hebrew words meaning more or less the same, 'big-hearted' or 'large-breasted', of which perhaps the crude contemporary compromise would be 'busty'. It is just possible too that Thaddaeus was an early miscopying of Theudas, the equivalent of Judas. In either case, Judas the son of James was distinguished from Judas Iscariot, in the Fourth Gospel, when both of them spoke to Jesus at the Last Supper. And if the lists of apostles are to be limited to the same twelve men, then a simple process of elimination demands the identification of Judas son of James with Thaddaeus. It is very possible that his friends graced him with

LEFT St Simon the Canaanite and (OVERLEAF) St Judas Thaddaeus, two portraits by Ribera (Spagnoletto) within the Prado Galley at Madrid. Each holds the symbol of his martyrdom, a stick, and a book.

the nickname of 'Busty Judas' to distinguish him from the 'traitor Judas', the last-named on all lists of the twelve.

It is, moreover, possible that the last *four* on the lists of apostles had something specific in common, for which they were regarded as a group. Certainly Judas Iscariot has been regarded by many scholars as the most passionate nationalist of the twelve, politically more shrewd than the rustic Galileans and more swift to perceive the political potential of Jesus as the long-awaited deliverer. It has even been possible to make out a case for Judas having been a Zealot commando or dagger-man (see page 203).

There is some documentary evidence that Judas Thaddaeus also was a Zealot. In two of the oldest manuscripts of the 'Apostolic Constitutions' – concerning the administration and structure of the early Church – he is described as 'Thaddaeus, also called Lebbaeus, who was surnamed Judas the Zealot'. This would seem to explain the only recorded conversation between Jesus and Judas Thaddaeus to be found in the Gospels.

Judas (not Iscariot) said to him, 'Lord, how is it that you will manifest yourself to us, and not to the world?' Jesus answered him, 'If a man loves me, he will keep my word, and my Father will love him, and we will come to him and make our home with him. He who does not love me does not keep my words; and the word which you hear is not mine but the Father's who sent me. These things have I spoken to you, while I am still with you. But the Counseller, the Holy Spirit, whom the Father will send in my name, he will teach you all things, and bring to your remembrance all that I have said to you. Peace I leave with you; my peace I give to you; not as the world gives do I give to you' (John 14:22–27a).

The setting is the Last Supper. There is an impending sense of final tragedy and the Zealot Thaddaeus still cannot understand why this need be so. He seems to be saying: 'It is not us whom you need to convince about your Messiahship, but the rest of the world. It is high time for a public demonstration of your power.' Jesus seems to reply as he did during his temptation: 'You cannot win men's love and loyalty by a display of force. Only when a man gives his heart will my Father and I be able to possess that man.' And finally, in direct contradiction to Zealot principles: 'My last wish for you is "peace", my own kind of peace that you will not achieve by worldly means.'

If the last three of the twelve on all lists were in fact Zealots, it may reasonably be deduced that the ninth member on all lists was also a Zealot, because these last four appear to be linked in a constant group, although the order of earlier names on the lists is varied. We may have very little certain historical information about the four men concerned – James the Less, son of Alphaeus, Simon the Zealot, Judas Thaddaeus and Judas Iscariot – but the convictions and history of the Zealot party are well and accurately recorded.

From Maccabean times in the first and second centuries BC to the fall of the fortress of Masada in the spring of AD 73 the term 'Zealot' was applied to those Jews who were impelled by a fanatical and nationalistic Messianism. Mattathias, the father of the Maccabees, had commissioned his sons: 'Now, my children, be zealous for the Law, and give your lives for the covenant of your fathers' (1 Macc. 2:50). Such men continued to follow the example of the Maccabean resistance to the efforts of the Selucid King Antiochus Epiphanes to force Greek culture and religion upon the Jews. They considered themselves to be the agents of God to deliver their nation from foreign oppressors under a banner of 'No rule but the Law – no King but God'. They became increasingly violent in their resistance both to the Roman occupation forces and to their own people who sympathized with Hellenism.

The Gospels include incidents involving the probable activities of the Zealot party. Among these is the report of certain Galileans 'whose blood Pilate mingled with their sacrifices'. Galilee, its climate and people, was fertile soil for discontent and revolt. There is a similar comment on some eighteen men who were killed when 'a tower in Siloam fell and killed them', probably while they were undermining some Roman fortifications. Jesus said of the Galileans: 'Do you think that those Galileans were worse sinners than all the other Galileans, because they suffered thus? I tell you, No; but unless you repent you will all likewise perish' (Luke 13:2–3). And of the other victims he said, 'Or those eighteen upon whom the tower in Siloam fell and killed them, do you think that they were worse offenders than all the others who dwelt in Jerusalem? I tell you, No; but unless you repent you will all likewise perish' (Luke 13:4–5).

Perhaps Barabbas, who was released by Pilate instead of Jesus, was a Zealot leader, a mistaken claimant for the Messiahship who left his followers to suffer while accepting his own release. The remark of one of the bandits crucified with Jesus implies a possible comparison between Barabbas and Jesus on his cross: 'Are you not the Christ, *save yourself and us!*' It would have been surprising if the Zealots had not at least considered the possible value of Jesus to their cause. John clearly says that the people wanted to make Jesus king in Galilee, and that his movements were restricted by the threat of such demonstrations.

The Jews who conspired to assassinate Paul at Jerusalem were almost certainly Zealots, acting in defence of the Law. 'When it was day, the Jews made a plot and bound themselves by an oath neither to eat nor drink till they had killed Paul. There were more than forty who made this conspiracy. And they went to the chief priests and elders and said, "We have strictly bound ourselves by an oath to taste no food till we have killed Paul"' (Acts 23:12–14).

Two unsuccessful uprisings are mentioned in the Acts of the Apostles (5:36), within the speech of the great Pharisee and Rabbi Gamaliel. The first

The Last Supper, a 15th-century mural in the Church of the Saviour at Paleochorio, Cyprus, painted by Philip Goul, suggestive of the conversation at the meal.

was led by Judas of Galilee, a Galilean peasant from Gamala who raised a revolt in bitter opposition to the census, or enrolment, ordered by the Roman Emperor, Augustus, during the governorship of Quirinius in AD 6. It was on the occasion of the incorporation of Judaea into the Roman province of Syria and it was probably the first Roman provincial census, by Roman methods, to be held in Judaea. The Galilean uprising was cruelly suppressed by the Romans, its leader Judas killed and two thousand of his followers crucified. The momentum, however, survived underground in the form of a constant guerrilla movement.

Judas the Galilean was the author of the fourth act of Jewish philosophy [whose members] agree in all things with the Pharisaic notions but they have an inviolable attachment to history, and say that God is their only Ruler and Lord. They do not mind dying any kind of death, nor do they heed the torture of their kindred and their friends, nor can any such fear make them call any man lord. And since this immovable resolution of theirs is known to a great many, I shall speak no further

OVERLEAF The fortress of Masada, last stronghold of the Zealots to fall in AD 73. The surrounding Roman vallum, the vast ramp up the west face of the rock, and the besieging General Silva's camp are in the foreground.

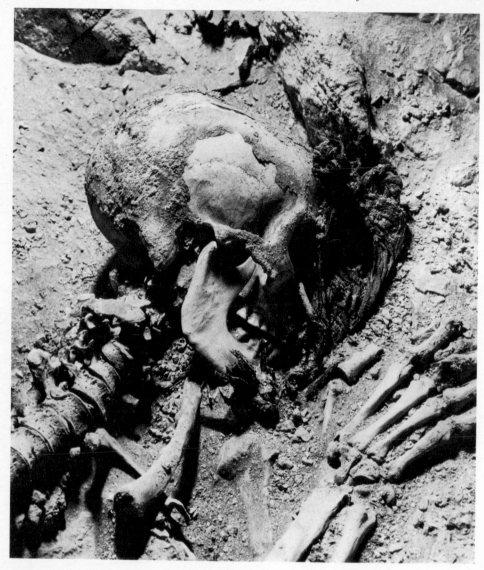

The Zealot garrison at Masada, rather than surrender to the Romans, destroyed itself by a mass suicide pact before the final attack.

about that matter; for I am not afraid that anything that I have said about them will be disbelieved, but rather fear that what I have said comes short of the resolution they show when they undergo pain (*The Antiquities of the Jews*, 18, 1, 6).

The other unsuccessful revolt quoted by Gamaliel was that of one Theudas and his four hundred followers in the early years of the first century. This may in fact have been the Theudas described by Josephus (*Antiquities*, 20.v.1) as having led a much larger rebellion in AD 44 or 45.

This party of fanatical nationalists was progressively taken over by extreme activists who, under the provocation of the increasingly repressive measures of successive Roman procurators, resorted to terrorism and brigandage. Such men banded themselves together into a group called the Assassins, or Sicarii, after *sica*, a dagger, which they concealed under their robes. This group attracted men of violence of all kinds, sworn to achieve their ends by the assassination both of the Romans and any of their countrymen willing to compromise with the occupation authority. Josephus had little good to say of them: 'Zealots, for that was the name these reckless persons went by, as if they were Zealous in good practices, and were not

The Turkish city of Urfa, seen from the ruins of the ancient city of Edessa, in whose archives the historian Eusebius found correspondence between Jesus and King Abgar (4 BC–AD 50).

rather extravagant and reckless in the worst actions' (*Wars of the Jews*, 4, 5, 9).

Such was the background of Simon the Zealot and probably that of Judas Thaddaeus, if not also of Judas Iscariot and of James the Less. It may be thought astounding that such men should have come to sink their differences in a common loyalty to their rabbi Jesus, to keep faith with him through his Crucifixion, to be present with the twelve at Pentecost and to carry his message of love into the Gentile world.

Beyond Pentecost, there is no further reference in the New Testament to Simon or to Judas Thaddaeus, but plenty of fascinating, legendary material, particularly the 'Acts of Thaddaeus' and a letter written to Jesus by Prince Abgar, ancestor of the Christian dynasty of Osrhoene. The name of Thaddaeus is linked with an ancient tradition centred round Edessa, a city now named Uria in Persian Mesopotamia. It is a popular legend in the Eastern Churches and goes back to the end of the second century. The story is to be found primarily in the *Ecclesiastical History* (1, 13) of Eusebius and the *Homily on Matthew* (10:4) by Jerome, whose source of information is admitted to be Eusebius.

This legend concerns an exchange of letters between one of the kings of Edessa, Abgar v (4 BC–AD 50). Eusebius claims to have extracted the correspondence from the archives of Edessa and to have translated it from the Syriac. The king, being ill, wrote to Jesus asking him to visit and heal him. Eusebius includes the title of the letter thus:

COPY OF A LETTER WRITTEN BY ABGARUS, THE RULER, TO JESUS AND SENT TO HIM AT JERUSALEM BY ANANIAS THE SWIFT COURIER.

Abgarus, ruler of Edessa, to Jesus the excellent Saviour who has appeared in the country of Jerusalem, greeting. I have heard reports of thee and of thy cures as performed by thee without medicine and without herbs. For it is said that thou makest the blind to see and the lame to walk, that thou cleansest lepers and casteth out impure spirits and demons, and that thou healest those afflicted with lingering disease, and raisest the dead. And having heard all these things concerning thee, I have concluded that one of two things must be true: either, thou art God, and having come down from heaven thou doest these things, or else, thou who doest these things art the Son of God. I have therefore written to thee to ask thee that thou wouldst take the trouble to come to me and heal the disease which I have. For I have heard that the Jews are murmuring against thee and are plotting to injure thee. But I have a very small yet noble city which is big enough for us both.

Jesus declined to come himself as he had been sent by God to Israel alone, but promised that after his Ascension he would send one of his disciples to Edessa to cure the king and preach the Gospel to the populace. Again, Eusebius includes the title of the reply:

THE ANSWER OF JESUS TO THE RULER ABGARUS BY THE COURIER ANANIAS.

Blessed art thou who hast believed in me without having seen me. For it is written concerning me that they who have seen me will not believe in me, and that they who have not seen me will believe and be saved. But in regard to what thou hast written to me, that I should come to thee, it is necessary for me to fulfil all things here for which I have been sent, and after I have fulfilled them thus to be taken up again to him that sent me. But after I have been taken up I will send to thee one of my disciples, that he may heal thy disease, and give life to thee and thine.

In one version of the story, a special blessing was added for the city of Edessa. Another later form (John of Damascus, *Orthodox Faith*, 4, 16) adds that when Jesus could not himself go to Edessa, he allowed Ananias to paint a portrait of him in order to take it by way of compensation to his royal master. When Ananias could not paint because of the brightness of Jesus's face, Jesus drew his headdress over his face and his portrait was miraculously printed on the cloth which Jesus then sent back to Abgar. The legend continues to tell that, following the Ascension of Jesus, Thomas sent Thaddaeus to Edessa where he stayed with a man called Tobias and healed many of the people. The king sent for Thaddaeus, who said: 'Because thou hast mightily believed in him that sent me, therefore have I been sent unto thee. And still further, if thou believest in him, the petitions of thy heart shall be granted thee as thou believest.' Abgar replied, 'So much have I believed in him that I wished to take an army and destroy those Jews who crucified him, if I had not been deterred from it by reason of the dominion of the Romans.'

Thaddaeus healed the king, who commissioned him to preach to the people. To this Thaddaeus replied:

I will preach in their presence, and sow among them the word of God, concerning the coming of Jesus, how he was born; and concerning his mission, for what purpose he was sent by the Father; and concerning the power of his works, and the mysteries which he proclaimed in the world, and by what power he did these things; and concerning his new preaching, and his abasement and humiliation, and how he humbled himself, and died and debased his divinity and was crucified, and descended into Hades, and burst the bars which from eternity had not been broken, and raised the dead; for he descended alone and rose with many, and thus ascended to his Father.

Thaddaeus's reply is a remarkable summary of the Christian creed and preaching of the early missionaries.

Copies of the letter of Jesus to Abgar and the portrait were used as local talismans. The letter has been found inscribed on a door lintel as far away as Ephesus very shortly after its composition. The letter was later used as a personal phylactery among the Anglo-Saxons, who declared 'it was a charm against lightning and hail and perils by sea and land, by day and by night and in dark places'. A more modern use of the Abgar correspondence is to be found in *West Sussex Superstitions*, a folk-lore record published in 1868:

An old woman in Tillington Parish keeps with religious care a printed copy of the apocryphal epistle of our Lord and Abgarus, King of Edessa, which she bought from a travelling man [i.e. pedlar], who told her that if she stuck it up on her kitchen wall, it would preserve her and her home from witchcraft and the evil eye.

The legend of Thaddaeus and Abgar is reported in various forms by Eusebius and in the *Doctrine of Addai*, a later work written in about AD 400, but the legend probably originated after the conversion of Abgar IX, 179–214. It was more accepted in the Eastern Churches than in the Western. In the Syriac tradition the founder of the Church at Edessa was called Addai, one of the seventy earliest disciples of Jesus. It may well be that this name is philologically the same as Thaddaeus, with whom Eusebius rightly or wrongly identifies him, substituting the Greek Thaddaeus for the Syrian Addai.

Eusebius wrote:

Thomas, under a divine impulse, sent Thaddaeus as herald and evangelist, to proclaim the doctrine of Christ to the king of the Osrhoenians (whose capital city was Edessa). When he came to these places, he both healed Abgarus (the King) by the word of Christ and astonished all there with the extraordinary miracles he performed. After having sufficiently disposed them by his works and led them to adore the power of Christ, he made them disciples of the Saviour's doctrine [teaching]. And even to this day, the whole city of Edessa is devoted to the name of Christ; exhibiting no common evidence of the beneficence of our Saviour likewise to them. And let this suffice, as taken from the accounts given in ancient documents.

Jerome confirms this identification and the *Apostolic Constitutions* equate Thaddaeus Lebbaeus and a 'Judas who preached in Edessa'. A second-century list of burial places of the apostles in Latin includes 'Judas-Thaddaeus in the castle (or square) at Edessa'. The word for 'castle', *beritha*, is more likely than Beryto, the seaboard town of Beyrut in this context, although Beyrut was a port on the Osrhoenian coast line.

Another legend which can be traced to the beginning of the fourth century linked Thaddaeus with his companion Simon the Zealot. This is to be found in the *Ten Books* of Craton, reputedly a disciple of Thaddaeus, who described the two apostles on missionary journeys throughout the vast Persian Empire. This is also confirmed in the *Apostolic History* of Abdias (6:7–21). From these two sources the story emerges that the two apostles Simon the Zealot and Judas Thaddaeus were strongly and constantly opposed by the Persian magi or priest-magicians, called Zaroes and Arfaxat.

Coins from the 1st and 2nd Jewish Wars, some bearing the inscription in Latin 'Judaea Capta'.

Despite this, the apostles won the confidence of the king, who imprisoned the magi and demanded their execution. At the request of the apostles, however, the magi were freed to conduct a slanderous campaign against the apostles. Simon and Judas Thaddaeus spent thirteen years preaching throughout the twelve provinces of the Persian Empire with enormous success, converting sixty thousand souls in Babylon alone.

On entering the city of Suanir they found that the seventy priests of the local temple and the whole populace had been incited by the magi to demand that the apostles sacrifice to the gods or die. The apostles explained that the sun and moon, whom the Persians worshipped as gods, were only the creations of the one true God whom they preached. Though the apostles drove the evil spirits out of the pagan idols in the form of two black and hideous figures who fled from the temple howling in blasphemy, the priests and people closed in on the apostles. Judas Thaddaeus said to Simon, 'I see

Symon apostolus

the Lord is calling us.' They died beneath a shower of stones and a battering of sticks – these two apostles are often therefore painted stick in hand.

The legend relates that the King Xerxes had the bodies of the two martyrs enshrined in the imperial capital within a new octagonal church consecrated on the third anniversary of the apostles' martyrdom, 1 July. The joint feast-day of St Simon and St Jude is today kept throughout the Western Church on 28 October.

When the first letter of Peter (3 : 13) refers to 'Zealous for what is right', there may well be an allusion to those 'good Zealots' Simon and Judas. For them the teaching of their Master not to resist evil and to love one's enemies must have had a very concrete application, rather than have been a counsel of perfection. Indeed Jesus's conception of his own kind of Messiahship, so far from that of the Zealots, must have evoked considerable contempt and acrimony. A possibly first-century 'Ode of Solomon' (28) personifies Jesus and clearly declared how he was hated, 'because I was *not* a Zealot'.

Judas qui ꞇ Tadeus apl's

The two Zealot apostles were martyred, at the instigation of
the priest-magicians of the city of Suanir in Persia, by a
rabble with sticks and stones – illustrations from the
Nuremberg Chronicle.

8 Thomas, 'Twin'

Thomas was that loyal and practical, down-to-earth, 'seeing-is-believing' disciple of Jesus, whose doubts of the Resurrection dissolved in the presence of his risen master. Thomas presents a fascinating problem of identity and relationship within the twelve, posed by his name and expressed in near-contemporary correspondence. Varying traditions claim the scenes of his missionary activity as Parthia and India. He is credited with an apocryphal Gospel which in fact dates from the second century.

Within the New Testament, in each of the Synoptic Gospels, the name of Thomas is included in the lists of apostles and in the roll of those who, in the Upper Room after the Ascension of Jesus, elected a replacement for Judas and received the Spirit at Pentecost. Nothing further is mentioned about him in the New Testament, outside the Fourth Gospel where he is called 'the Twin'. John, however, mentions four different occasions when the presence of Thomas was significant to the Gospel story. From these four passages the character of Thomas emerges with some force.

The first occasion was when Jesus had been hounded out of Jerusalem to seek safety in some quiet village, possibly Ephraim, among the hills several miles to the north of the city and overlooking the wilderness of Judaea. Suddenly the news of the illness of Lazarus of Bethany arrived; Jesus at once decided to go back to him at Bethany, within two miles of Jerusalem. This seemed a peculiarly rash decision, and Thomas was frightened. He knew well the danger involved, but volunteered to accompany him, in very blunt if realistic terms: 'Let us also go, that we may die with him.' Thomas, the realist and the pessimist, was also a man of loyalty and courage.

The second incident took place at the Last Supper, in the upper room on the Western Hill, on Maundy Thursday night. Jesus had been preparing his disciples for his coming departure, 'And when I go and prepare a place for you, I will come again and take you to myself, that where I am you may be also. And you know the way where I am going' (John 14:3–4). Thomas at once interrupted him, 'Lord, we do not know where you are going; how can we know the way?' (John 14:5).

St Thomas, according to his apocryphal Acts, was a builder and carpenter by trade, hence the set-square in his hand in this portrayal by Rubens, in the Prado Gallery, Madrid.

It was not as though the others knew any more than Thomas, but he was not the sort to let his master get away with something that he, Thomas, did not understand. No doubt Christians should be thankful for Thomas's question, which evoked such an answer. 'Jesus said to him, "I am the way, and the truth, and the life; no one comes to the Father but by me. If you had known me, you would have known my Father also; henceforth you know him and have seen him."' Thomas was not the sort of man to live patiently with his doubts, without expressing them in order to resolve them. Jesus's answer did not attempt to convince the bewildered Thomas, but to call forth the personal loyalty of which Thomas indeed had so much.

The third occasion was in the same room, but after the Resurrection of Jesus. On the Easter night, Thomas had not been with the others when Jesus first came to them and when the others had told him, Thomas had not been able to believe them. Perhaps he felt they had succumbed to wishful thinking or had seen a ghost. His reply to them was quite typical of the man. 'Unless I see in his hands the print of the nails, and place my finger in the mark of the nails, and place my hand in his side, I will not believe' (John 20:25).

A week later, the disciples were again all together in the Upper Room and this time Thomas was with them. Though the doors were barred for fear of the Jews, again Jesus was there. Thomas's doubts and demands provided both Jesus and the evangelists with just the opportunity that was needed, to bring home the reality of the Resurrection to the disciples both then and now. Jesus called Thomas over to touch the scars of crucifixion: 'Put your finger here, and see my hands; and put out your hand, and place it in my side; do not be faithless, but believing' (John 20:27).

In that moment Thomas must have seen both the body on the cross, hanging by hands and feet, the side opened by the soldier's spear, *and* his living friend and master. As these two figures fused together, so Thomas leapt the gap between the loyalty to a friend and an adoring faith in that friend as God himself. His doubts disappeared and he identified his friend as both 'My Lord and my God!'

The gratitude of the Christian Church for Thomas's obstinacy is recorded in the collect for his feast in the Anglican Book of Common Prayer, which interprets the event as a providential confirmation of the Resurrection of Jesus.

The final reference to Thomas is among the seven disciples who went fishing on the Lake of Galilee, when at dawn they met Jesus on the shore, and landed a miraculous draught of fish. Thomas is mentioned only second to Simon Peter in this final post-Resurrection story of Jesus. He expressed no doubts this time but was by now a highly respected and integrated member of the company.

The name of 'Thomas', or 'Thomas called Didymus' as the Fourth

Detail of a pulpit by Guido of Como in St Bartholomew's church, Pistoia, near Florence, shows the Risen Jesus and the unbelief of Thomas.

Gospel calls him, poses the whole question of his place and relationship within the company of the twelve. The word 'Didymus', to be found in the King James version, is not a surname any more than Thomas, but a Greek translation of the Hebrew 'Thomas'. Both mean 'twin'. From the New Testament, this apostle's real name is not known, but among the Jews he was called 'Thomas' and among the Greek Christians – mostly in Asia Minor perhaps – he was called 'Didymus'. 'Thomas' and 'Didymus' are both one name, or nickname, of the same meaning in different languages.

179

The question is whether the name 'Thomas' or 'Didymus' in the first century was already in conventional use and applied to people who were not really twins. 'Twin' and 'Twining' (son of a twin) are English surnames today; Oliver 'Twist' derives from 'twiced'. The French *Jumeau*, the German *Zwilling* and the Scottish *Gemmell* (deriving from the Latin *Gemellus*) are accepted surnames. In the orient where there are no hereditary surnames, it is more likely that the Hebrew form 'Thomas' implied a personal characteristic. The Greek form 'Didymus', however, appears to have been used very early as a surname. In AD 79, the Oxythyncus Papyrus (243) exhibits a mortgage in which one of the parties is 'Didymus, the son of Serapion, the son of Didymus'. Similarly in the Amherst Papyrus (66), there is a murder trial before 'Claudius Didymus also called Geminus', in AD 124. Such illustrations indicate a colourless surname rather than a real twin-naming. When did the Hebrew form 'Thomas' similarly lose its original meaning and what was his personal name?

Eusebius tells us that Thomas, one of the twelve, sent to Edessa Thaddaeus, who succeeded in converting the king Abgar and his whole city. Eusebius bases the whole story (which is told in chapter 7 of this book) upon a Syriac document that he found in the archives of Edessa and which he quotes thus. 'After the Ascension of Jesus, Judas – who is also called Thomas – sent to him the apostle Thaddaeus.' The name 'Judas Thomas' is again found in the Syriac *Doctrine of Addai*: 'After that Jesus had ascended to heaven, Judas Thomas sent to Abgar Addai the Apostle. . . .' Among the Syrians, therefore, Thomas was known as 'Judas the Twin', as also in the apocryphal Acts of Thomas, where the two names clearly refer to one person. For instance: 'Whilst Judas was reasoning thus, our Lord appeared to him in a vision of the night, and said to him "Fear not, Thomas!"'

If the real name of Thomas, as the Syriac scriptures and Edessan legends indicate, was Judas, then who was his twin brother? The reference to Judas as 'the twin' would imply that the other 'twin' was the more important of the two. On the face of it, this could only have been one of the more important of the twelve apostles, but they would seem to be all excluded. With the brothers of Bethsaida, the sons of Zebedee and the sons of Alphaeus, the name of Judas is not mentioned; nor could it have been Nathaniel Bartholomew, for he already had a single patronymic (son of Talmai).

The Syriac Acts of Thomas give a surprising answer, ranking Judas Thomas as none other than the twin of Jesus himself, an equation clearly unacceptable to the Catholic Church, which maintains the Virgin Birth. Even though the Edessan writers were Ebionite in belief, rejecting the Virgin Birth, it is more likely that they linked wishfully and almost unconsciously their own founder Judas Thomas with Judas, the 'brother' of the Lord who may also have been the writer of the General Epistle of Jude.

The Acts of Thomas also relate the twinship or similarity between Jesus

St Thomas, detail from a 15th-century mural of the Apostles in the church of the Holy Cross, Platanistasa, Cyprus, by Philip Goul.

and Judas Thomas both in their appearance and in their work of salvation. In the first Act of Thomas, a young bridegroom 'saw the Lord Jesus in the likeness of the apostle Judas Thomas, who shortly before had blessed them and departed from them, conversing with the bride, and he said to him: "Didst thou not go out before them all? How art thou now found here?" But the Lord said to him: "I am not Judas who is also Thomas, I am his brother."' This same twin-like similarity is emphasized in the story of the demon with the woman. The demon asks Judas Thomas: '"What have we to do with thee, apostle of the Most High. . . . Why art thou like God thy Lord, who hid his majesty and appeared in the flesh . . . art thou, then, born of him?"' And again, in the sixth Act, the woman rescued from hell by Jesus describes him to Judas Thomas as 'the one who is like thee'. It is this form of twin-ship of appearance that is to be found in the medieval Roman breviaries, where Thomas is described as *simillimus salvatori*, because he was 'likest to our Saviour'.

Yet another possible explanation of the twin-ship of Jesus and Thomas is that they discovered in later life that they had been born on the identical day, though of different parents!

Perhaps the wisest solution to the problem of the identity of Thomas and his relationship within the apostolic college is to accept the brotherhood or similarity but not his natal twinship to Jesus. He can then be identified with the Judas mentioned by both Mark (6:3) and Matthew. '"Is not this the carpenter's son? Is not his mother called Mary? And are not his brothers James and Joseph and Simon and Judas? And are not all his sisters with us?"' (Matt. 13:55, 56a).

Although the Fourth Gospel (7:3–5) emphasizes that the brothers of Jesus did not at first believe in him and wanted him to seek greater publicity in Jerusalem, they were later fully accepted into the circle of apostles after the Ascension. In fact they were included with Mary the mother of Jesus immediately following the list of apostles, and they probably took part in the election of the substitute apostle, Matthias. 'All these with one accord devoted themselves to prayer, together with the women and Mary the mother of Jesus, and with his brothers' (Acts 1:14). Very soon, James the eldest brother of Jesus had become a pillar of the primitive Church in Jerusalem, and Paul declared that the risen Jesus had appeared specially to his brother, James (1 Cor. 15:7). In the list of the seven apostles greeted by the risen Jesus on the shore of Galilee (John 21:2), Thomas follows directly on the name of Peter.

There is no doubt of the subsequent respect in which the apostles held the family of Jesus. James was revered as 'the Just' and Judas may well have been named 'the twin' for his closeness of companionship, as well as his looks, to Jesus. Following the end of the Jewish War and the disastrous fall of Jerusalem, the Romans hunted down all Jews of the royal stock of David. This policy continued under the Emperors Vespasian and Domitian. The descendants of Judas were denounced as of the line of David and, as the family concerned both believed and boasted, directly related to the Messiah.

Concerning the travels of Thomas, there are two traditions which are not necessarily wholly contradictory. The biblical scholar Origen of Alexandria and Asia, quoted by Eusebius of Caesarea, propounds the tradition that when the apostles divided the world into missionary areas Parthia fell by lot to Thomas (*Ecclesiastical History* 3:1). A lady pilgrim, known as Sylvia of Aquitaine, who visited Edessa at the end of the fourth century, said that Jesus had promised to send Thomas to evangelize the city

Parthian horseman, an ancient bronze of Syrian or Iraqi origin, now in the British Museum. Parthian cavalry played a large part in the defeat of Roman legions in the 1st century.

and that Thomas's complete body was still preserved there.

Edessa was the capital of Osrhohen in northern Mesopotamia, between the Tigris and the Euphrates, within the curl of and some miles from the latter. The Latin historian Crosius would hardly include Edessa within Parthia, which he described as bounded on the east by the river Indus and on the west by the Tigris, on the north by the Caucasus and the Caspian Sea, on the south by the Persian Gulf. The area included some thirty-two tribes living in wild and mountainous country, dominated from the centre by the rugged strength of the untamed Parthians, who were respected even by Rome. Yet it is far beyond Parthia and the Indus that the second tradition of Thomas takes us, right down into south India.

There are those who discount the possibility of the apostle Thomas reaching India, or who say that there were many 'pseudo-Indias' in his day. Whether or not the Byzantines erroneously called all non-white races Indians, from Ethiopia to Arabia to Ceylon, from the time of Alexander's crossing of the Indus, the Greeks and then the Romans knew the way to India. Alexander left a viceroy in the Punjab to rule 'fifteen tribes, five thousand considerable cities and villages without number'. His fleet sailed down the Indus, along the coast and up the Persian Gulf while he marched across the desert to meet them at Susa. Although Alexander died at Babylon in 323 BC, he had crossed the barrier of the Persian Empire to link his people with India. As well-informed writers, Ptolemy, later king of Egypt, Alexander's generals, and admirals, pilots, navigators and military staff gave to the western world a reasonably truthful idea of India's position and physical features.

In the years that followed, the Ptolemies and Seleucids exchanged ambassadors with the Indian kings; political and numerical relationships were maintained until the rise of a new Parthian Empire at the turn of the second century BC. Communications between the Mediterranean and the Indus remained disrupted and the Parthians held the Romans at bay on the banks of the Euphrates until the Augustan age. In AD 5, the historian Strabo described the sea route to India: 'I was with Gallus at the time he was prefect of Egypt, and accompanied him as far as Syene [on the Upper Nile] and the

Feluccas on the Upper Nile on the sea-route to India, from which travellers made a land passage to the Red Sea on their way round Oman to the Indian Ocean.

Mirani Fort on the treacherously rocky coastline of the Bay of Muscat, for centuries the haunt of fierce tribesmen and unscrupulous pirates.

frontiers of Ethiopia. I found that about one hundred and twenty ships sail from Myos-Hormos [on the Red Sea] to India [along the coast of Arabia and across the Persian Gulf].'

As Christianity spread in the west and religious freedom was granted by the Emperor Constantine, a convert in the early part of the fourth century, Christians began to take part in trade with distant countries, frequenting many eastern markets. They sought out their fellow-Christians in different eastern tribes and provinces, gathering details about the beginning and growth of their faith in those far-off lands and reporting their findings to those at home. Thus information about the Eastern churches began to find a place in the writings of the patristic fathers from the fourth century onwards.

Gregory of Nazianzen (329–390) wrote the following about Thomas: 'What? Were not the apostles strangers amidst the many nations and countries over which they spread themselves, that the Gospel might penetrate into all parts . . .? Peter indeed may have belonged to Judaea, but what had Paul in common with the Gentiles, Luke with Achaia, Andrew with Epirus, John with Ephesus, Thomas with India, Mark with Italy?' Ambrose of Milan (333–397) was thoroughly acquainted with the Greek and Latin classics; he had, too, a considerable knowledge of India and her peoples, gained from first-hand reports of travelling scholars. He wrote of the Indian Ocean, the River Ganges, of Persia, Ethiopia and the deserts of Arabia. He did not confuse India with other countries. About Thomas, he wrote 'Even those kingdoms shut out by rugged mountains became accessible to them, as India to Thomas, Persia to Matthew . . .'.

Pilgrims bathing at dawn in the River Ganges at the holy city of Benares, to which Ephesus, as the cathedral city of ancient paganism, has been compared.

Pepper plantations at Kuching, Sarawak. It was the Roman demand for pepper and spice from Malabar which stimulated trade between India and the Mediterranean.

Jerome, the erudite Latin Father, had a detailed knowledge of India, culled from the classical and patristic writings. He gives the overland route from Mauritania to India, 'passing through Africa, Egypt, Palestine, Phoenicia, Coelen Syria, Osrhohen, Mesopotamia and Persia'. He gives the Red Sea route to southern India:

The sailors of the Red Sea . . . arrive at the city of Auxum [Aden] after many difficulties and perils. On both shores live nomads and even ferocious beasts. Always on the lookout and always armed, they carry food for the whole year. The sea is full of hidden rocks and rough shoals, so that the lookout . . . sits on the high mast, giving orders how to steer and turn the ship. Happy the voyage that after six months reaches the port [of Aden] where the open sea begins. It takes almost a year to reach India and thence to the river Ganges. The chief port to which the Romans came at this time was Muziris, situated in the pepper country of Malabar [the south-west coast of India].

The doorway into the throne hall at Persepolis. The carving shows the King giving audience above ranks of Persian and Median guards.

About Thomas, Jerome wrote 'He [Jesus] dwelt in all places: with Thomas in India, with Peter in Rome, with Paul in Illyricum, with Titus in Crete, with Andrew in Achaia, with each apostolic man in each and all countries.'

Isidore of Seville, at the turn of the sixth century, says 'This Thomas preached the Gospels of Christ to the Parthians, the Medes, the Persians, the Hercanians and the Bactrians – and to the Indians of the oriental region and penetrating the innermost regions. Sealing his preaching by his passion, he died transfixed with a lance at Calamina, a city of India, and there was buried with honour.' Isidore's list of peoples certainly marks the overland trail from the Euphrates to the Indus, from one side of the Parthian Empire to the other.

If the Greek and Latin Fathers accepted the double tradition of Thomas's mission to Parthia and India, other evidence has to be found for the localities of his work in India. The early third-century Syrian document of the apocryphal Acts of Thomas is of interest here. The gist of this work is that Thomas came to India, preached the Gospel in the kingdom of a certain Gudnaphar (Goundophorus in Greek, Gundophorus in Latin), and converted the king and many of his subjects. Thomas then moved on to another kingdom, where he converted the queen and some of her people, but the king of this land, Mazdai (Mizdaios in Greek, Misdeus in Latin), was jealous and ordered the assassination of the apostle.

The Acts are considered a Christian (and in places heretical) variety of the Hellenistic–Oriental romance, with a skilful use of historical figures and colourful narrative taking the story back into the first century. It is the

Armenia, land of lakes and mountains south of the Caucasus, converted by Gregory the Illuminator in the 3rd century, claims to have received the gospel from Bartholomew and Thomas.

Tribal dispositions from
a Map by Ptolemy c.150

1 BARBARIA	10 MESOPOTAMIA
2 AZANIA	11 ARMENIA
3 ETHIOPIA	12 ASSYRIA
4 LIBYA	13 SUSIANA
5 EGYPT	14 MEDIA
6 PETRAEA	15 PERSIA
7 SYRIA	16 HYRCANIA
8 ARABIAN	17 PARTHIA
DESERT	18 KARMANIAN
9 BABYLONIA	DESERT
	19 KARMANIA
	20 MARGIANA
	21 ARIA
	22 DRAGIANA
	23 CEDROSIA
	24 BACTRIANA
	25 PAROPAMIS
	26 ARACHOSIA

Towns and Trade-routes from the
West to India in the First and

The martyrdom of St Thomas, from William Caxton's
'Golden Legend', 1493. The Acts of Thomas describe his
despatch by soldiers with lances, on a hill outside the city.

typical tale of the journey of a hero into a foreign wonderland, linking his life with historical figures of that period, relating his fantastic works of power and finally his heroic sufferings and martyrdom. The story appears to illustrate the lively cultural and commercial relationships between Syria and India, but to have little basis in historical fact, despite its entertainment value.

In the first half of the nineteenth century, some thirty thousand coins were found in Afghanistan and the Punjab, a good many of them belonging to the period of the Indo-Parthian King Gondophares. His name in Greek characters of various spellings was on the obverse of these coins which must have been minted in the first half of the first century. Later in the nineteenth century, a block of stone in the north-east of Peshawar and now in Lahore museum revealed an inscription dated in the twenty-sixth year of the reign of a King 'Gunuphara'. Some scholars linked the three sources, the Acts, the coins and the inscription, to indicate that Thomas might have visited the Punjab, although there is no certain link between Thomas and Gondophares.

In the Ethiopic version of the Acts, the writer says that the King of Gona (probably Mysore on the south-east coast of India) had invited Thomas to the 'south country' also mentioned in the Acts. Roman coins of the reigns of the Emperors Tiberius and Caligula found at Bangalore indicated the communications between Rome and Mysore in the first century. It is therefore not impossible that a Mysore rajah named Kutnappar (Gudnaphar) should have invited Thomas to India.

Another theory equates 'King Mazdai' (who according to the Acts was responsible for the apostle's death) with a Tyrrhenian King of Mylapore, on the east coast. The earliest documentary evidence for a possible link between Thomas and Mylapore dates from the thirteenth century. Mar Solomon of Basora, in the Book of the Bees, says, 'Thomas taught the Indians and because he baptized the daughter of the king, he was stabbed to death with a spear. Habban the merchant brought his body and laid it at Edessa . . . others say that he was buried at Mahlaph, a city in the land of the Indians.' Marco Polo, the Venetian traveller, actually visited the tomb and wrote, 'The body of Saint Thomas the Apostle lies in the province of Maabar, at a certain little town having no great population.'

From the fifteenth century references become more clear and specific: 'Proceeding onwards Nicolo [de Conti, a travelling merchant], arrived at a maritime city which is named Malepur. . . . Here the body of St Thomas lies honourably buried in a large and beautiful church.' A letter from four Nestorian bishops refers to the 'house of St Thomas the Apostle' (presumably the church over the tomb), situated 'in a city on the sea named Meliapor, in the province of Silan'. From the time of the Portuguese in the sixteenth century, Mylapore has been a southern suburb of the city of Madras.

In 1630, a life of Francis Xavier described how 'the holy man of God, Thomas, came to preach to the city of Calamina, which people of the place call Meilapore'. A number of earlier writers had mentioned Calamina as the scene of Thomas's martyrdom, a name which probably derived from the Syrian pilgrims' use of their Syriac word *galmona*, meaning a rocky hillock. The Acts describe the death of Thomas 'outside the city on a mountain', and an eastern synaxarium, or history of the saints, says that 'five soldiers took the apostle up the mount and covered him with wounds'. When the tomb at Mylapore was excavated in 1523, the priest in charge recorded on oath the finding of 'some bones of the skull' and of the spine, 'an earthen vessel' and a 'spearhead entirely of Malabar iron, having the shape of an olive leaf and stuck in a portion of a wooden shaft . . .' at the place corresponding to the thigh.

There are in fact three traditions linking Thomas with three different parts of India: with the Punjab on the upper reaches of the Indus in the north-west, with the Coromandal coast and the cities of Madras and Mylapore in the east, and finally with the Kerala (Malabar) coast on the

This gothic cathedral of St Thomas, at Mylapore in the suburbs of Madras, consecrated in 1896, enshrines a traditional tomb of the Apostle Thomas.

south-west, around the port and lagoons of Cochin. This last tradition is not based on any early documentary evidence but upon the strong oral family traditions handed down to succeeding generations of the 'St Thomas Christians', as they call themselves, to this day.

This Mar Thoma Church, the Christian community in Malabar, is first mentioned by Cosmas Indicopleutes during the sixth century, in his *Christian Topography*. Cosmas writes, 'In the island of Taprobane, in the interior of India where the Indian Ocean is, there is a Church of Christians; there are also clergy and faithful ... likewise too in Male as it is called, where the pepper grows.' Male was one of the great ports on the Malabar coast, having five separate pepper markets. Cosmas goes on to write about the clergy and congregation at Malabar. It is not surprising that there should be Christian communities along that coast-line, for Muziris (now Kodungallur) was the chief port at which the Romans landed, marking the end of the great sea lane to India. By the time of Augustus, it was already a large city with its own imperial temple. If Thomas ever travelled by sea, to or from India, he would have berthed on the Malabar coast at Muziris.

When the Portuguese landed in the sixteenth century, they recorded the traditions and customs of the Christians, whom they found south of Goa. Both Christians and Hindus told of the preaching of Thomas, who had converted many of the Brahmins, though others retained their own religion and left the district. Thomas is said to have established Christian communities in seven different localities in Malabar. From the sixth to the sixteenth century they were under the ecclesiastical jurisdiction of the Patriarch of Babylon, who never challenged the apostolic origin of the Malabar Church. In one of these localities north of the Cochin lagoons, called Palayur, within the modern church compound are still to be found all the paraphernalia of Hindu worship there in bygone days, including the sacrificial well. At Palayur too there is the 'Jew's Hill', the site of an early Jewish settlement whose community Thomas the Jew might well have visited.

The memory of the apostle is still kept alive in the minds of the St Thomas Christians by their traditional songs, recording the exploits of their founder. The Ramban Song reflects the theme of the Acts of Thomas, while the marriage songs – sung by Hindus at Christian feasts and marriages – extol the coming, teaching and martyrdom of Thomas. The songs refer to the local Christians as the 'Nazrani', the Nazarenes, as the earliest Christians were called. The link between the Malabar and the Mylapore Christians is one of pilgrimage to the traditional tomb of the apostle, now in the gothic cathedral of St Thomas in Mylapore, consecrated in 1896.

The apocryphal writings linked with the apostle are not limited to the Acts alone. The fourth-century 'Gospel of Thomas' is not a Gospel in the usual sense, but a very extensive collection of sayings – many of them parallel to but not identical with the scriptural sayings of Jesus. Eusebius

St Joseph's church, Vipon Island, in the Cochin Lagoon. The Christian community in Malabar has been linked with the Apostle Thomas since the 6th century.

described this work as 'commanded by the heretics, under the name of the Apostle Thomas'. Only since 1945 has a complete text of the Gospel been available, following its finding in Egypt, where it is now preserved in the Coptic Museum in Old Cairo.

The 'Infancy Story', reputedly by an 'Israelite Philosopher' Thomas, depicts Jesus as an infant prodigy before the age of twelve. It is full of fanciful and playful miracles, crudely and vividly told in very bad taste. This fairytale approach does away with the necessity of any normal human development of the child Jesus. The 'Apocalypse of Thomas', perhaps a fifth-century work as it refers to the Emperor Theodosius, is reminiscent of the apocalyptic passages in the Gospels of Mark (chapter 13), of Matthew (chapter 24), and also in the Revelation of St John the Divine (chapters 6–9).

By far the most interesting work is the 'Acts of Thomas'. This is a clearly intended clothing of the apostolic story in legend and half-history. Although condemned by early scholars like Augustine of Hippo as heretical, it was soon 'purged' and absorbed into Catholic usage. It is a strange but entertaining mixture of narrative, hymnody and liturgy – calling for the transformation of evil into good – and the direction of the Christian soul from earthly appetite to union with the heavenly Lord.

At the same time, regardless of the truth or fiction of the Indian tradition, the Acts paints a real picture of the character of the apostle. Judas Thomas may well have been a carpenter like his father and perhaps like his 'half' brother Jesus. He was certainly a man who did not avoid his responsibilities nor turn his back on his doubts or difficulties. Indeed he went right through them, up to the hilt of the lance that killed him. Jesus's parable of the two sons well illustrates the attitude and calibre of Thomas. The father asked both boys to go and work in his fields; the first agreed but never went, the second refused but went. Such was Thomas, an instinctive pessimist whose first reaction was inevitably to demur, but who never failed to face a challenge and, once convinced, to pursue his purpose with the same dogged perseverance with which he had at first rejected it. However historical the Indian tradition or the saga of Acts which illustrates it, the central character is life-size, a man of the same iron purpose and courageous humility as his brother and master, Jesus.

The Acts opens with the story of Thomas being sold by his master to an Indian merchant called Abban, who takes him to India and leases his services as a carpenter to the rajah.

At that time we apostles were all in Jerusalem; and we divided the regions of the world, that each one of us might go to the region which fell to his lot, and to the nation to which the Lord sent him. India fell to Judas Thomas, who is also [called] Didymus; but he did not wish to go, saying that through the weakness of the flesh he could not travel, and: 'How can I, who am a Hebrew, go and preach the truth among the Indians?'

And as he thus spoke and thought, it happened that a certain merchant was there who had come from India. His name was Abban and he had been sent by King Gundaphorus, and had received orders from him to buy a carpenter and bring him back to him.

Now the Lord saw him walking in the market-place at noon, and said to him: 'Dost thou wish to buy a carpenter?' He said to him: 'Yes.' And the Lord said to him: 'I have a slave who is a carpenter, and wish to sell him.' And when he had said this he showed him Thomas from a distance, and agreed with him for three pounds of uncoined silver, and wrote a deed of sale saying: I Jesus the son of Joseph the carpenter confirm that I have sold my slave, Judas by name, to thee Abban, a merchant of Gundaphorus the king of the Indians. And when the deed of sale was completed the Saviour took Judas, who is also [called] Thomas, and led him to the merchant Abban. And when Abban saw him, he said to him: 'Is this thy master?' And the apostle in answer said: 'Yes, he is my Lord.' But he said: 'I have bought thee from him.' And the apostle was silent.

On the following morning the apostle prayed and besought the Lord, and said: 'I go wither thou wilt, Lord Jesus; thy will be done!' And he went off to Abban the merchant, carrying with him nothing at all, save only his price. For the Lord had given it to him, saying: 'Let thy price also be with thee, with my grace, whithersoever thou goest!'

But when the apostle came to the cities of India with Abban the merchant, Abban went off to salute King Gundaphorus, and reported to him concerning the carpenter whom he had brought with him. The king was glad, and commanded that he should come to him. So when he came the king said to him: 'What kind of trade dost thou understand?' The apostle said to him: 'Carpentry and building.' The king said to him: 'What craftsmanship, then, dost thou know in wood, and what in stone?' The apostle said: 'In wood, ploughs, yokes, balances, pulleys, and ships and oars and masts; and in stone, pillars, temples and royal palaces.' And the king said: 'Wilt thou build me a palace?' And he answered: 'Yes, I will build and finish it; for this is why I came, to build and work as a carpenter.'

And the king took him and went out of the gates of the city, and began to discuss with him on the way the building of the palace and how the foundations should be laid, until they came to the place where he wanted the building to be. And he said: 'I wish the building to be here.' And the apostle said: 'Yes, for this place is suitable for the building.' But the place was wooded, and there was much water there. So the king said: 'Begin to build.' But he said: 'I cannot begin to build now at this season.' And the king said: 'When canst thou?' And he said: 'I will begin in November and finish in April.' But the king said in astonishment: 'Every building is built in summer, but thou canst build and establish a palace even in winter?' And the apostle said: 'So it ought to be, and there is no other way.' And the king said: 'Well then, if this is thy resolve, draw me a plan how the work is to be, since I shall come back here [only] after some time.' And the apostle took a reed and drew, measuring the place; and the doors he set towards the east, to face the light, and the windows to the west towards the winds, and the bakehouse he made to be to the south, and the aqueduct for the service to the north. But when the king saw it, he said to the apostle: 'Truly thou art a craftsman, and it is fitting for thee to serve kings.' And leaving much money with him he departed from him.

And at appointed times he used to send his money and what was necessary both for his own sustenance and for that of the other workmen. But he took it all and dispensed it, going about the towns and the villages round about, distributing it and bestowing alms on the poor and afflicted, and he gave them relief, saying: 'The king knows that he will receive a royal recompense, but the poor must for the present be refreshed.' After this the king sent an ambassador to the apostle, writing to him thus: 'Show me what thou hast done, or what I should send thee, or what thou dost require.' The apostle sent to him, saying: 'The palace is built, and only the roof remains.'

But when the king came to the city he inquired of his friends concerning the palace which Judas who is also Thomas was building for him. But they said to him: 'Neither has he built a palace, nor has he done anything else of what he promised to do, but he goes about the towns and villages, and if he has anything he gives it all to the poor, and he teaches a new God and heals the sick and drives out demons and does many other wonderful things; and we think he is a magician. But his works of compassion, and the healings which are wrought by him without reward, and moreover his simplicity and kindness and the quality of his faith, show that he is righteous or an apostle of the new God whom he preaches. For continually he fasts and prays, and eats only bread with salt, and his drink is water, and he wears one garment whether in fine weather or in foul, and takes nothing from anyone, and what he has he gives to others.' When he heard this, the king smote his face with his hands, shaking his head for a long time.

And he sent for the merchant who had brought him, and for the apostle, and said to him: 'Hast thou built me the palace?' And he said: 'Yes, I have built it.' The king said: 'Then when shall we go and see it?' But he answered him and said: 'Now thou canst not see it, but when thou dost depart this life thou shalt see it.' But the king in great wrath commanded both the merchant and Judas who is also Thomas to be put in bonds and cast into prison until he should investigate and learn to whom the king's money had been given, and so destroy him together with the merchant. But the apostle went rejoicing into prison, and said to the merchant: 'Fear nothing, but only believe in the God who is preached by me, and thou shalt be freed from this world but from the age to come shalt obtain life.' Now the king was considering with what manner of death he should destroy them. But when he had resolved to flay them alive and then burn them with fire, in the same night Gad the king's brother fell sick, and because of the pain and disappointment which the king had suffered he was greatly depressed. And he sent for the king.

And as they conversed the soul of Gad his brother departed. The king mourned Gad deeply, for he loved him greatly, and commanded him to be buried in royal and costly apparel. But when this happened, angels took the soul of Gad the king's brother and carried it up to heaven, showing him the palaces there and the dwellings and asking him: 'In what kind of palace wouldst thou live?' But when they drew near to the building of Thomas the apostle, which he built for the king, Gad when he saw it said to the angels: 'I pray you, sirs, allow me to live in one of these lower apartments.' But they said to him: 'Thou canst not live in this building.' And he said: 'Why?' They said to him: 'This palace is the one which that Christian built for your brother.' But he said: 'I pray you, sirs, allow me to go to my brother, that I may buy this palace from him. For my brother does not know of what kind it is, and will sell it to me.'

Then the angels let Gad's soul go. And while they were putting the grave clothes on him, his soul entered into him; and he said to those who stood around him: 'Call to me my brother, that I may ask of him one request.' So at once they brought the good news to the king, saying: 'Thy brother is alive again!' The king sprang up and came with a great crowd to his brother, and going in he stood by the bed as if stupefied, unable to speak to him. But his brother said: 'I know and am persuaded, brother, that if anyone asked of thee the half of thy kingdom, thou wouldst have given it for my sake. Wherefore I beseech thee to grant me one favour which I ask of thee. Sell me that palace which thou hast in heaven.' And the king said: 'Whence should I have a palace in heaven?' But he said: 'The one the Christian built for thee, who is now in prison – the man the merchant brought thee after buying him from one Jesus. I mean that Hebrew slave whom thou didst wish to punish, as having suffered some deception at his hand – against whom I too was vexed, and died, and now I am alive again.'

Then the king, considering the matter, understood [his words] concerning the eternal goods which were more excellent for him and which he was to receive, and said: 'That palace I cannot sell to thee, but I pray that I may enter it and live in it, and be counted worthy [to belong to] its inhabitants. But if thou dost truly wish to buy such a palace, behold the man is alive, and will build thee one better than that.' And immediately he sent and brought the apostle out of the prison, and the merchant who had been shut up with him, saying: 'I entreat thee, as a man entreating the servant of God, to pray for me and beseech him whose servant thou art, that he forgive me and overlook the things that I have done against thee, or thought to do, and that I may become a worthy inhabitant of that dwelling for which I did not labour at all, but thou didst build it for me labouring alone, the grace of thy God working with thee, and that I too may become a servant, and serve this God whom thou dost proclaim.'

But the apostle, possessed [with] joy, said: 'I praise thee, Lord Jesus, that thou hast revealed thy truth in these men. For thou alone art the God of truth, and no other; and thou art he who knows all that is unknown to the many; thou, Lord, art he who in all things shows mercy and forbearance to men.'

Thomas, at their own request, anointed and baptized the king and his brother. On the following day, after a vision in the night, Thomas determined to bring the brothers into full membership of Christ's Church, so he 'laid his hands upon them and blessed them. And breaking the bread of the eucharist he gave it to them, saying: "This eucharist shall be to you for compassion and mercy, and not for judgement and equital." And they said, "Amen."'

The final Act describes the establishment by Thomas of the Christian faith and Church within quite another community. Here it is the queen who responds and is converted, while the jealous king Misdaeus (or Mazdai) opposes the apostle.

Misdaeus was considering in what manner he should put him to death; for he was afraid of the crowd which stood around, since many believed him, and even some

of the leading people. And rising up he took Judas with him outside the city; and a few armed soldiers followed him. But the crowds supposed that the king wished to learn something from him; and they stood and observed him. But when they had advanced three stadia, he handed him over to four soldiers and one of the officers, commanding them to take him to the mountain and despatch him with spears. And he himself returned to the city. And when he had prayed, he said to the soldiers: 'Come and fulfil [the command] of him who sent you!' And at once the four soldiers smote him and slew him. But all the brethren wept. And wrapping him in fine robes and many fine linen cloths they laid him in the tomb in which the kings of old [were buried].

After a long period of witness by the Christians, the king's son fell ill and the king turned for help to the God of the Christians.

And when his son was in this manner restored to health, he [Misdaeus] came together with the other brethren, becoming submissive to Siphor [the Christian presbyter]. And he besought all the brethren to pray for him, that he might find mercy from our Lord Jesus Christ.

The Acts of Judas Thomas are completed, which he wrought in the land of the Indians, fulfilling the command of him who sent him, to whom be glory for ever and ever.

The figure of St Thomas, the builder and carpenter, set-square in hand, in the great Basilica of St John Lateran, in Rome.

9 Judas Iscariot

The story of Judas Iscariot, more than that of any other member of the twelve, has gathered accretions and interpretations. Not only was this so during the lapse of time between the events and their recording but, ever since, the character and motive of the traitor have constantly been under analysis. But it is not possible with any certainty to draw from the Gospels a single and concurrent account of Judas's position and status among the twelve.

In the Synoptic Gospels he does not appear until the Passion, except in the lists of apostles, where he always comes last and with a qualifying epithet. In Mark and Matthew this is 'who betrayed him'; in Luke it is 'who became a traitor'. All four Gospels refer to him as Judas 'Iscariot' and the Fourth Gospel calls him 'Judas, the son of Simon Iscariot, for he, one of the twelve, was to betray him'. The implication is that the term 'Iscariot' applied equally to his father as to Judas, but what that term means is not absolutely certain.

'Iscariot' might have been an Aramaic adaptation of the word for a dagger-man, in Latin *sicarius*, in Greek *sicarios*, derived as has already been mentioned from *sica*, a short curved dagger carried at the waist, similar to that found among the Kurds today. These *sicarii* developed as a guerilla group within the patriotic Zealot party; they were pledged to expel the Romans by violence, assassination and terrorism. This would make both father and son fanatical partisans, with nationalistic hopes of liberation by the establishment of a Messianic kingdom, to be fulfilled perhaps in the person of Jesus of Nazareth.

Another even more far-fetched theory links 'Iscariot' (Scariot in the Syrian manuscripts) with the Greek *scortia*, meaning a leather jacket, the purse-like pockets of which might have been useful to any itinerant treasurer such as Judas. The simpler and more credible interpretation of the term 'Iscariot' is *Ish* (Hebrew for 'man of') *Kerioth*, a village in the hills of Judaea, from which both father and son could have come. This would

'The Kiss of Judas', detail from a fresco by Giotto in the Chapel of the Scrovegni family, at Padua.

indeed make Judas the 'man of Kerioth', the only southerner among the twelve. As a Judaean he might well have been a more sophisticated, more shrewd and more dispassionate character among a bunch of rustic, emotional and impassioned Galileans. And, in fact, he was the 'odd man out' – essentially lonely, maligned and misunderstood.

John frankly calls him a 'thief' or 'betrayer', 'possessed by the devil', or 'the son of perdition'. It is as if the evangelists could not paint him black enough in retrospect. After all, they had all at one time or another denied or deserted their master and the blackness of Judas might make their own greyness less noticeable. Jesus himself, however, is acknowledged to have been a clear reader of personality and he must have first called Judas and then have appointed him as the treasurer or accountant of the little company. The very fact that he was his rabbi's choice to be treasurer of the band of disciples shows that he could be trusted with an important office. Jesus is hardly likely to have given Judas the job if it was to be a source of temptation to him, nor is Judas likely to have joined a band of itinerant and penniless preachers if he was a greedy and petty pilferer. Jesus must have seen in Judas a potentially useful member of his team, and Judas must have seen in Jesus the potential fulfilment of Messianic prophecy.

Christians, particularly in the west, have long speculated on the reasons for the original choice of Judas, his suicide, his motives and the relatively small amount of blood-money paid to him. The explanation, offered by John in the Fourth Gospel, that Judas was impelled by sheer greed and that he was completely lacking in integrity is far from convincing. Another theory is that Judas the Judaean was swift to recognize the potential of Jesus, 'mighty in works and deeds', to be the true Messiah so long awaited by such as Judas.

Judas, more than the others perhaps, seems to have misunderstood or disregarded Jesus's interpretation of his own Messiahship. Faced with a slow and steady process of disillusionment and disappointment, at what so many of Jesus's followers considered to be lost opportunities (John says they wanted to make him 'king'), Judas's impatience seems to have grown until he himself grasped the initiative.

Whether intending perhaps to force Jesus into declaring himself Messiah, at the height of the Passover feast, when support was ready to hand, or whether driven to a pathetic revenge for his deep personal disappointment and frustration, Judas acted the traitor. Three years' close acquaintance with Jesus may well have convinced Judas of Jesus's Messiahship, but also of a genuine inability to declare himself. Judas, by pushing Jesus at the tactical moment, may well have felt that he was acting for Jesus's own good; for Judas's ideal of Messiahship did not include Jesus actually allowing himself to be killed. Once, however, the plot was under way, there was no brake to apply.

OPPOSITE 'Judas receives the price of betrayal', by Giotto in the Chapel of the Scrovegni family, at Padua.

A 12th-century mural in St Martin's church, Zillis, Switzerland, depicts Judas declaring Jesus's innocence and returning the thirty pieces of silver, to be told 'That is your concern!'

All three Synoptic Gospels declare that Judas himself approached the chief priests 'in order to betray Jesus to them'. They were glad and promised to reward him. Matthew adds that they gave him thirty silver pieces, the equivalent of under ten dollars or four pounds sterling – that is, the purchase-value of a foreign slave in Old Testament times, or the amount claimed by a Jewish slave if his master drew blood in New Testament times. If Judas was as greedy as is often supposed, he could have extorted far more from the high priests.

At the Last Supper with his disciples, the night before the Passover feast, Jesus gave a clear warning of his impending betrayal: 'And as they were at table eating, Jesus said, "Truly, I say to you, one of you will betray me, one who is eating with me." They began to be sorrowful, and to say to him one after another, "Is it I?" He said to them, "It is one of the twelve, who is dipping bread in the same dish with me. For the Son of Man goes as it is written of him, but woe to that man by whom the Son of Man is betrayed! It would have been better for that man if he had not been born"' (Mark 14:18–21). Matthew adds that Jesus identified Judas as his betrayer. 'Judas, who betrayed him, said, "Is it I, Master?" He said to him, "You have said so"' (Matt. 26:25).

The Fourth Gospel, substituting the story of the feet-washing for that of the Last Supper, describes the conversation that followed in considerable detail. The warning is all the more poignant, following the lesson in humility illustrated by Jesus's washing of his disciples' feet, including those of Judas. 'Truly, truly, I say to you, a servant is not greater than his master; nor is he who is sent greater than he who sent him. If you know these things, blessed are you if you do them. I am not speaking of you all; I know whom I have chosen; it is that the Scripture may be fulfilled. "He who ate my bread has lifted his heel against me"' (John 13:16–18).

It is not difficult to reconstruct the Last Supper scene, with the guests reclining full length round the table, three to each divan, according to custom leaning on the left arm and eating with the right. The host was likely to be in the centre of one couch, while the places on either side of him on the same divan were the coveted places of honour. On his right side, the nearest guest was half-turned away from, but could lean back closer to, his host. This is just what 'the disciple whom Jesus loved' did: 'When Jesus had thus spoken, he was troubled in spirit, and testified, "Truly, truly I say to you, one of you will betray me." The disciples looked at one another, uncertain of whom he spoke. One of his disciples, whom Jesus loved, was lying close to the breast of Jesus; so Simon Peter beckoned to him and said, "Tell us who it is of whom he speaks." So lying thus, close to the breast of Jesus, he said to him, "Lord, who is it?" Jesus answered, "It is he to whom I shall give this morsel when I have dipped it." So when he had dipped the morsel, he gave it to Judas, the son of Simon Iscariot' (John 13:21–26).

In the other place of honour, on Jesus's left and on the same couch, was Judas Iscariot in easy reach of Jesus's right hand. If it was the Passover meal, the 'morsel' could well have been the sop normally handed to a guest as a mark of honour. This could consist of a minute sandwich of unleavened bread – similar to a water biscuit – containing a pinch of bitter herbs and dipped in a 'fruit and nut' paste, of the appearance and consistency of mud. At each Passover, together with the shank-bone of the Passover lamb, these three items would be out on the table under the candlelight. They were there to remind the family of the Passover story, when there was no time for the bread to rise, when the Israelites were forced to make mud bricks without straw in their bitter slavery in Egypt.

Judas accepted the sop, but rejected Jesus's last gesture of friendship, and at once indicated that he was going to leave the table. Whereupon Jesus quietly screened his departure and Judas, literally and figuratively, slipped

The path round the corner of the city wall across the Roman bridge over the Kedron, which Judas probably took to enter the Garden of Gethsemane.

out into the dark: 'Then after the morsel, Satan entered into him. Jesus said to him, "What you are going to do, do quickly." Now no one at the table knew why he had said this to him. Some thought that, because Judas had the money box, Jesus was telling him, "Buy what we need for the feast"; or, that he should give something to the poor. So, after receiving the morsel, he immediately went out; and it was night' (John 13:27–30).

The Synoptic Gospels go on to describe the walk down to Gethsemane, the Agony in the Garden, and then the arrival of Judas with the temple police. Judas had given them a sign by which they would recognize Jesus: '"The one I shall kiss is the man; seize him and lead him away safely." And when he came, he went up to him at once, and said "Master!" And he kissed him. And they laid hands on him and seized him' (Mark 14:44–46). The kiss on the hand was the normal greeting of the disciple for his rabbi. Luke says that when Judas arrived at the head of the crowd 'he drew near to Jesus to kiss him', but that Jesus probably stopped him with the question, 'Judas, would you betray the Son of man with a kiss?' Both Mark and Matthew, however, representing an earlier tradition, use a word for kiss that means 'kissed him fondly and repeatedly' – something very different from a traitor's kiss, as though Judas was already in the throes of remorse.

The description of the arrest in the Fourth Gospel is rather one of purposeful surrender. 'Then Jesus, knowing all that was to befall him, came

OPPOSITE The Risen Jesus invites the seven fishermen-apostles to share his breakfast by Galilee. A 19th-century stained-glass window in the nave of Lincoln cathedral.

forward and said to them, "Whom do you seek?" They answered him, "Jesus of Nazareth." Jesus said to them, "I am he." Judas, who betrayed him, was standing with them. When he said to them, "I am he," they drew back and fell to the ground. Again he asked them, "Whom do you seek?" And they said, "Jesus of Nazareth." Jesus answered, "I told you that I am he; so, if you seek me, let these men go"' (John 18:4–8).

Judas is not mentioned at the Trial before the Council, though he must have given his evidence, probably of Jesus's acceptance of the title of Messiah from Peter at Caesarea Philippi: 'Thou art the Christ'. But it required two witnesses to convict and Peter himself contrived to remain out of sight in the gallery, partially recognized by his Galilean accent in spite of his denial. Again Judas is mercifully not mentioned at the later trial before Pilate, or at the Crucifixion, though his presence and his feelings are all too clearly revealed in the events that followed.

Matthew's account of Judas's pathetic remorse and suicide is based on the Old Testament prophecy of Zechariah (11:12, 13): 'When Judas, his betrayer, saw that he was condemned, he repented and brought back the thirty pieces of silver to the chief priests and the elders, saying, "I have sinned in betraying innocent blood." They said, "What is that to us? See to it yourself." And throwing down the pieces of silver in the temple, he departed, and he went out and hanged himself' (Matt. 27:3–5). Luke's account of an accidental death, known to all the people in Jerusalem, seems more likely to be accurate.

Peter's speech to the apostles recounts how Judas himself bought a field and met with an accident in it: 'Falling headlong he burst open in the middle, and all his bowels gushed out.' This could perhaps mean suicide, either by hanging himself or throwing himself over the cliff of the Western Hill, on to the rocks in the valley below. It could mean that he was run over by a wagon, as an early apocryphal writer describes, in a manner which crushed and burst his body open. Both accounts, however, link the death of Judas with a cemetery for foreigners in Jerusalem, called Akeldama, 'the Field of Blood'. There are still the tombs of crusaders on the site which is to be seen today, south of the Western Hill, across the Valley of Hinnom.

What was Judas's real motive? Outside the Passion story there are only two incidents which have any link with Judas and both of these are to be found in the Fourth Gospel. The first follows the Feeding of the Five Thousand, when Jesus evaded the efforts of those who wanted to 'make him king' and escaped into the wilderness. From that moment some of his disciples drifted away and Jesus asked the twelve whether they were going to leave him. Then, when Peter on their behalf affirmed his loyalty, Jesus asked, 'Did I not choose you the twelve, and one of you is a devil?' The evangelist explained this as referring to Judas Iscariot, who was going to betray him.

Was it in fact Jesus's reluctance to declare his Messiahship which pre-

The Betrayal and Arrest, a small 16th-century bas-relief in alabaster, four by five inches, and framed in velvet, from the Silberstein Collection, Cincinnati.

S·IOHANNES · ANDREAS · S·BARTHOLOMAEVS

ABOVE The route from the Betrayal within the Garden of Gethsemane in the background, past the Maccabean tombs in the Kedron Ravine, to the Trial in the high priest's palace.

cipitated Judas's action, in a last desperate effort to force his hand at the height of the Passover festival? Perhaps Judas, like his namesake of Galilee, was indeed a Zealot, who like Martin Luther King had a dream, and he saw that his dream would be crucified so long as it remained a dream of love rather than practical politics. He may even have felt that he was helping his master to reveal his true purpose for Israel. Perhaps Judas was the only one of the twelve with the political foresight to grasp the coming catastrophe of the Galilean revolt unless the Messiah were to come soon.

LEFT Detail from the Last Supper by Andrea del Costagno, in the San Apollonia, Florence. Judas symbolically is the only one on the opposite side of the table.

ABOVE The suicide of Judas, carved in relief on a 12th-century stone capital at Autun Cathedral in Burgundy.

The second incident is that concerning the anointing of Jesus by Mary of Bethany and Judas's rather prim reaction: '"Why was this ointment not sold for three hundred denarii and given to the poor?"' (John 12:5). What is most significant, however, is the evangelist's comment on that reaction. 'This he said, not that he cared for the poor but because he was a thief, and as he had the money box he used to take what was put into it' (John 12:6). The colloquial Greek leaves no doubt that John accused Judas of both greed and theft, for the word used for 'take' meant 'pilfer' or 'filch'.

This was a direct and rather unworthy indictment of their treasurer as exploiting his office for his own gain. This motive projected into the Passion story simply does not seem to fit the fact of Judas's selection by Jesus as a disciple, nor his appointment as treasurer, presumably for his business acumen. This is not to deny the evil inspiration which, as John says, was the basic cause of Judas's treachery. Though this incident may reflect some retrospective mud-slinging on the part of the evangelist, it may also illuminate a clash of relationships between Judas and the majority of the twelve. This might perhaps have been particularly the case with the one who reclined at supper so affectionately on the other side of Jesus. Judas was not one of the inner circle, and the shrewd and ambitious Judean disciple might well have been jealous of what he regarded as his rustic rivals from the north. Nor would it have been surprising if the disrespect had been mutual between the competent but frustrated businessman with political ambitions, and those enthusiastic and idealistic 'sons of thunder'.

As was to be expected on the subject of Judas, the apocryphal writings have little to say that is either kind or constructive. They tend to project back into the life of Judas the contemporary assessment of him within the Church at the time of writing. They add little or nothing factual to the character or motive of Judas. The fragment of a late Arabic Gospel of the Infancy of Jesus describes how, as a child, he was hit by the child Judas and drove the devil out of Judas 'in the form of a dog'. In a possibly fifth-century Coptic fragment of the Gospel of Bartholomew, Judas's wife is said to have induced her husband to treachery. The same idea is to be found in a fantastic legendary 'Acts of Pilate' of about the same date, in which Judas says:

'Rise up, wife, and provide me a rope, for I would hang myself, as I deserve.' But his wife said to him: 'Why sayest thou such things?' And Judas saith to her: 'Know of a truth that I have wickedly betrayed my master Jesus to the evil-doers for Pilate to put him to death: but he will rise again on the third day, and woe unto us!' And his wife said to him: 'Say not nor think not so; for as well as this cock that is roasting on the fire of coals can crow, just so well shall Jesus rise again, as thou sayest.' And immediately at her word that cock spread his wings and crowed thrice. Then was Judas yet more convinced, and straightway made the halter of rope and hanged himself.

Christendom very early saw in Judas all the evil instincts of mankind and imputed to him faults of which the New Testament knows nothing. For early Christians, the story of Judas held a kind of dreadful fascination. The late second-century bishop of Hierapolis, Papias, added yet another story of the death of Judas from a disease from which he swelled until his belly burst and his bowels were scattered. Very few indeed had a kind word to say for Judas, but more recent writers have asked what Judas's own friends at Kerioth would have said for him, and what Jesus might have said. If Jesus had met him halter in hand, would he not have stopped him with a gentle touch? Would there not have followed a passionate prostration, repentance and forgiveness, and even another kiss?

A 15th-century mural of Pentecost by Philip Goul in the Church of the Saviour, at Paleochorio, Cyprus. Judas was replaced by Matthias to make up the Twelve.

10 Matthias, the Substitute

Matthias was the twelfth apostle, elected to fill the gap left by the death of the traitor Judas. Following the Ascension of Jesus, the apostles returned from the Mount of Olives to the Upper Room on the Western Hill, which was to become their headquarters. There, in the presence of some hundred and twenty disciples of Jesus, Peter outlined the brief ministry of Judas Iscariot among the twelve and recorded his violent death. He then called for the replacement of Judas from among the men who had been associated with the first disciples, from the Baptism of John to the Ascension of Jesus. It was important that there should be twelve apostles, to witness to the fact of the Resurrection of Jesus. There had to be twelve to correspond to the twelve tribes of Israel. Indeed, in some ancient manuscripts a tribe is assigned to each apostle. 'So one of the men who have accompanied us during all the time that the Lord Jesus went in and out among us, beginning from the baptism of John until the day when he was taken up from us – one of these men must become with us a witness to his resurrection' (Acts 1:21–22).

The necessary qualifications were his human witness of the Resurrection and his divine selection, so two certain witnesses were proposed of which one was chosen by lot, after earnest prayer for the guidance of the Holy Spirit. This method had been used for the selection of Saul as the first king of Israel, a thousand years previously. 'And they put forward two, Joseph called Barsabbas, who was surnamed Justus, and Matthias. And they prayed and said, "Lord, who knowest the hearts of all men, show which one of these two thou hast chosen to take the place in this ministry and apostleship from which Judas turned aside, to go to his own place." And they cast lots for them, and the lot fell on Matthias; and he was enrolled with the eleven apostles' (Acts 1:23–26).

Tradition numbers both candidates among the seventy disciples sent out two by two, during the early ministry of Jesus, but neither of them is mentioned elsewhere in the New Testament, nor is there any certain knowledge of their subsequent ministries. Paul, the apostle to the Gentiles, refers in the

A 19th-century engraving of St Matthias holding the symbol of his martyrdom, a butcher's cleaver. He was traditionally the Apostle to the Man-eaters.

Corinthian correspondence (1 Cor. 15 : 5–6) to the Resurrection appearance of Jesus to the twelve, after his appearance to Peter and before his appearance to a larger group of some five hundred disciples. The Alexandrian scholar Origen (*c*. Cels II. 65) considered that on this occasion the twelve included Matthias. This does not preclude the possibility that Matthias had been previously one of the seventy.

It would be surprising if there had not been some confusion in the apocryphal literature between the names of the two apostles Matthew and Matthias. This occurs in the writings of Clement of Alexandria, who refers to them both as vegetarians! Clement also says that other writers equate Zacchaeus the tax-collector, mentioned in Luke's Gospel (19:1–10), with Matthias, as though he too was a tax-collector. This would accord with the Coptic text of the 'Book of the Resurrection of Christ' by Bartholomew, which describes Matthias as the rich man who 'forsook all to follow Jesus' – an obvious reference to the call of Matthew, the tax-collector (Matt. 9:9).

Clement does, however, preserve three quotations from a second-century Hebrew-Christian Gospel of Matthias, listed as on a par with the Gospel of Thomas by Origen of Alexandria, Eusebius of Caesarea, Ambrose and Jerome of Rome and even by the Venerable Bede. These are the three

An 11th-century Byzantine ivory panel of the Ascension of Jesus, showing the Apostles surrounding Mary his mother.

St Matthew and St Luke, inspired by angels, independently begin to write gospels.
Painted by Philip Goul, AD 1466, in the Church of the Holy Cross, Platanistasa, Cyprus.

The Spirit in the form of a dove and flames descends upon Peter, Mary and the Apostles, while the Jerusalem populace gathers outside. A mural by Giotto, at Florence.

sayings attributed to Matthias: 'Wonder at what is present, establishing this as the first step to the knowledge of things beyond.' 'To strive with the flesh and misuse it without yielding to it in any way to unbridled lust, but to increase the soul through faith and knowledge.' 'If the neighbour of one of the chosen sin, then has the elect sinned; for if he had so conducted himself as the Word commends, the neighbour would have had such awe at his way of life that he would not have fallen into sin.'

A sixth-century apocryphal 'Acts of Andrew and Matthias' relates that at the partition of the world among the apostles, the land of the cannibals (literally 'man-eaters') fell to Matthias as his missionary sphere. On his arrival there, Matthias was blinded and cast into prison, where his eyesight was miraculously restored and he was rescued by Andrew. It was long thought that this work might have been an excerpt from the earlier 'Acts of

Andrew', but it has been clearly shown not to be linked with that work. It is rather one of a whole cycle of similar tales of wonder which originated in Egypt from the sixth century. This particular story was told in verse by Cynewulf some three centuries later, within the Anglo-Saxon poem 'Andreas', which is still preserved today. It is indeed Andrew who is the hero of the story and whose adventures continue in a later sequel, 'The Acts of Peter and Andrew'.

At that time all the apostles were gathered together and divided the countries among themselves, casting lots. And it fell to Matthias to go to the land of the anthropophagi. Now the men of that city ate no bread nor drank wine, but ate the flesh and drank the blood of men; and every stranger who landed there they took, and put out his eyes, and gave him a magic drink which took away his under-standing. So when Matthias arrived he was so treated; but the drink had no effect on him, and he remained praying for help in the prison. And a light came and a voice: 'Matthias, my beloved, receive sight.' And he saw. And the voice continued: 'I will not forsake thee: abide twenty-seven days, and I will send Andrew to deliver thee and all the rest.' And the Saviour went up into heaven. Matthias remained singing praises; when the executioners came to take victims, he kept his eyes closed. They came and looked at the ticket on his hand and said: 'Three days more and we will slay him.' For every victim had a ticket tied on his hand to show the date when his thirty days would be fulfilled.

When twenty-seven days had elapsed, the Lord appeared to Andrew in the country where he was teaching and said: 'In three days Matthias is to be slain by the man-eaters; go and deliver him.' 'How is it possible for me to get there in time?' 'Early tomorrow, go to the shore and you will find a ship.' And he left him.

After a miraculous voyage steered by Jesus in the form of a pilot, past sphinxes and synagogues, Andrew at last arrived outside the city of the 'man-eaters'.

Jesus reassured him and told him what trials awaited him in the city, and en-couraged him to endure them, and departed. They entered the city, unseen, and went to the prison. The seven guards fell dead at his prayer; at the sign of the cross the doors opened. He found Matthias and they greeted each other. Andrew looked at the victims, who were naked and eating grass, and smote his breast and re-proached the devil: 'How long warrest thou with men? Thou didst cause Adam to be cast out of paradise: thou didst cause his bread that was on the table to be turned to stones. Again, thou didst enter into the mind of the angels and cause them to be defiled with women and madest their savage sons to devour men on the earth, so that God sent the flood. . . .' Then they both prayed, and they laid their hands on the prisoners and restored first their sight and then their sense, and Andrew bade them go out of the city and remain under a fig-tree and await him: there were two hundred and seventy men and forty-nine women. And Andrew commanded a cloud, and it took Matthias and the disciples and brethren to the mount where Peter was teaching, and there they remained.

The Conversion of St Paul, by Michelangelo, within
the Vatican Chapel of St Paul, implies the direct
intervention and proclamation 'I am Jesus whom you
are persecuting'.

Part 3

THE APOSTOLIC COMMUNITY

. . . Fellow citizens with the saints and members of the household of God, built upon the foundation of the apostles and prophets, Christ Jesus himself being the corner-stone, in whom the whole structure is joined together and grows into a holy temple in the Lord; in whom you also are built into it for a dwelling place of God in the Spirit.

(Letter of Paul to the Ephesians 2 : 19–22)

St Luke, the Evangelist, his pen, scroll and symbol of the ox. An illuminated illustration from a medieval manuscript of his Gospel in Greek.

11 From the Pen of Luke

The Greek *apostolos* means literally 'messenger'; in nautical parlance it could mean a 'ship under sail' or 'captain of an expedition'. The Hebrew equivalent of 'one sent', *shalish*, carries the additional meaning of an 'agent', bearing not only the message and authority of the sender but even his presence to the addressee. During his Galilean ministry, Jesus had sent the twelve disciples on a local mission. 'And he called to him the twelve, and began to send them out two by two, and gave them authority over the unclean spirits. He charged them to take nothing for their journey except a staff; no bread, no bag, no money in their belts; but to wear sandals and not put on two tunics. And he said to them, "Where you enter a house, stay there until you leave the place. And if any place will not receive you and they refuse to hear you, when you leave, shake off the dust that is on your feet for a testimony against them"' (Mark 6:7–11).

After the Resurrection, all four Gospels describe an apostolic commission to be the witnesses (literally martyrs) for Jesus throughout his world. Matthew refers to the 'twelve apostles' (10:2) and the Seer of Patmos envisages the foundations of the heavenly city as marked with 'the twelve names of the twelve apostles of the Lamb' (Rev. 21:14). Despite the defection of Judas and the denial of Peter, there was a considerable continuity between the twelve disciples and the twelve apostles who were to form the nucleus of the Christian community in Jerusalem.

The Gentile Luke, with world-wide ambitions for the Christian Gospel, is concerned to show the Church's mission to the world as the extension of Jesus's mission to Israel. This leads Luke to limit his idea of apostleship to the twelve chosen disciples of the Galilean ministry. Furthermore, Luke describes Peter explaining to the family of the Roman centurion Cornelius how the twelve had set about their mission to all who would listen. 'And Peter opened his mouth and said: "Truly I perceive that God shows no partiality, but in every nation any one who fears him and does what is right is acceptable to him. And we are witnesses to all that he [Jesus] did both in

The Stoning of Stephen, outside the walls of Jerusalem, in the presence of Saul. An event symptomatic of the persecution of Hellenist Christians. By Westlake.

the country of the Jews and in Jerusalem. They put him to death by hanging him on a tree; but God raised him on the third day and made him manifest; not to all the people but to us who were chosen by God as witnesses, who ate and drank with him after he rose from the dead. And he commanded us to preach to the people, and to testify that he is the one ordained by God to be judge of the living and the dead"' (Acts 10:34, 35, 39–42).

How right was Luke to credit with the initiation and conduct of a concerted Gentile mission the twelve Jewish companions of Jesus's lifetime, rather than some later Gentile converts following perhaps the apostolic lead of Peter and John? There is no sound evidence for any general mission by the twelve, not even a continuation of Jesus's mission to his own people. Perhaps, in the early years following the Ascension, this is not so surprising, for Jesus's original commission to the twelve had been emphatic, even if in oriental hyperbole: 'Go nowhere among the Gentiles, but rather go to the lost sheep of the house of Israel.' The specific number of the twelve was closely linked with the idea that the Christian movement represented a renewal of Israel, hence the twelve disciples corresponding to the twelve tribes. It is as the founders of the renewed Israel that the twelve have been immortalized and, in the judgement, they are appointed to sit on twelve thrones judging the twelve tribes of Israel.

The memory of those twelve was so important to the early Christian Church because they had been uniquely close to Jesus during his lifetime. Paul claimed that the risen Jesus had appeared specially to the twelve. They were the apostles *par excellence* and founder members of the Church, yet they were not primarily missionaries, bishops or even local leaders of the primitive Church. What then was their role? For perhaps twenty years after the Ascension they acted as a council to make decisions for the future and growth of the Church. During this time, there seem to have been two major policy decisions recorded in the Acts.

The first crisis arose in about the year 36, through friction between Jewish and Greek Christians over the poor relief in Jerusalem. The Hellenists complained that their poor did not get a fair share in the distribution of food and clothing. This almost certainly reflected a deeper quarrel between those Jewish Christians who conformed to the demands of the Law and the temple, and the Greek Christians who did not. The wise decision of the council of the twelve was to appoint seven assistants from the Greek congregation, in order to give the Hellenists their own leaders.

When the Christians in Jerusalem were persecuted by the Jewish authorities, it was not surprising that it was the Greek congregation who suffered most and were scattered in all directions beyond the borders of Judaea. Stephen's impassioned indictment of the Jewish authorities for failing to observe the spirit of the Law and for their reliance on the worship of the temple reflected something of the Hellenistic protest against the

Detail from a Raphael cartoon of St Paul preaching at Athens. The Acts records his invitation by, but his failure to impress, the Athenian philosophers.

Judaisers within the Christian community. During their persecution, the Jewish Christians, including presumably the twelve, virtually escaped attention, while the Greek Christians fled from Judaea to become Christian missionaries throughout the Mediterranean world. One of them, Philip the Evangelist, converted the entire Samaritan community and then sent word to the twelve in Jerusalem, who despatched Peter and John officially to confirm and establish the Church in Samaria.

The second critical decision to come before the council of the twelve in Jerusalem was necessitated, in about the year 49, by the acceptance of Gentiles into the new Christian community at Antioch. The mass conversions by Barnabas and Paul of non-Jews seemed to threaten the good relationships between the Christian movement and Judaism. Again the council acted with wisdom and generosity by ratifying Paul's policy and making the minimum demands upon Gentile converts.

On each of these two occasions, the method of making the decisions was important. The twelve called the whole local congregation together before presenting a proposal for action. In the case of the Greek leadership, the congregation selected and presented candidates of their own choice to the twelve. In the council of Jerusalem, Paul and Barnabas presented their case not only to the council of apostles but to the elders as well. With the support of Peter, they returned with an authoritative apostolic decree. 'It seemed good to the apostles and elders, with the whole Church', to select Judas and Silas to accompany them and to lay upon new converts 'no greater burden than was absolutely necessary'. Thus, the twelve acted as a council to confer with the congregation, in exactly the same manner as in the Essene community at Qumran where it was the custom of the council to consult the 'Assembly of the Many'.

To sum up the structure of the apostolic community to be found in the Acts, there were first the 'apostolic men' such as the twelve, Barnabas and Paul, also James the brother of Jesus and elected president of the Church in Jerusalem. Secondly, there were the local elders (Paul calls them overseers at Ephesus), appointed by the apostolic men after the manner of synagogue elders. Then lastly, there were the *ad hoc* appointments to supply a particular need in a particular situation. Among these last, the most important by far were the seven ministers, and the least important the envoys or escorts of the apostles. The words translated 'overseers', 'elders' and 'ministers', in the Greek *episcopoi*, *presbuteroi* and *diaconoi*, refer to their function rather than their office, even though these words have been adopted to express the threefold ministry of bishops, priests and deacons. Their various functions were the administrative and pastoral oversight and the serving of the practical needs of their community. Of the detailed functions of the twelve apostles, apart from those of Peter and to a lesser extent of John, the Acts has very little to offer.

12 From the Experience of Paul

The letters of Paul present a marked contrast to Luke's writings. Whereas Luke suggests that the apostles were a closed corporation of twelve governing the whole Church, Paul disagrees, claiming his own apostleship to be as valid as any of the twelve and extending the apostolate to a rather wider circle. Paul in fact separates the twelve from the apostles, when he lists the post-Resurrection appearances of Jesus. 'For I delivered to you as of first importance what I also received, that Christ died for our sins in accordance with the scriptures, that he was buried, that he was raised on the third day in accordance with the Scriptures, and that he appeared to Cephas, then to the twelve. Then he appeared to more than five hundred brethren at one time, most of whom are still alive, though some have fallen asleep. Then he appeared to James, then to all the apostles. Last of all, as to one untimely born, he appeared also to me' (1 Cor. 15:3–8).

The relationship between the twelve and the apostles in the primitive Church is far from clear. On Paul's first visit to Jerusalem in the year 39, he spent fifteen days in Jerusalem with Peter, but 'saw none of the other apostles except James the Lord's brother' (Gal. 1:19). Less than ten years after the Ascension had the twelve, as an institution, ceased to function? Certainly Paul knew no authority of the twelve, apart from the apostles, of whom Peter was the recognized leader. Perhaps the twelve had been absorbed into the group of apostles whom Paul refers to as travelling missionaries, often accompanied by their wives and usually supported by the congregations they visited.

Some fourteen years after his first visit, Paul returned to Jerusalem with Barnabas and Titus, for the council's decision on the admission of Gentile Christians. On that occasion he was welcomed by James, Peter and John, whom he described as 'reputed to be pillars'. Of these, James the brother of Jesus had replaced James, the son of Zebedee, to make up the triumvirate of apostles, Peter, James and John, who had belonged to the inner circle of the twelve. Paul remarked that this James had been honoured with a special

St Paul the Apostle to the Gentiles; 12th-century mural in the Church of Panyia Tou Arakou at Lagoudera Monastery, Cyprus.

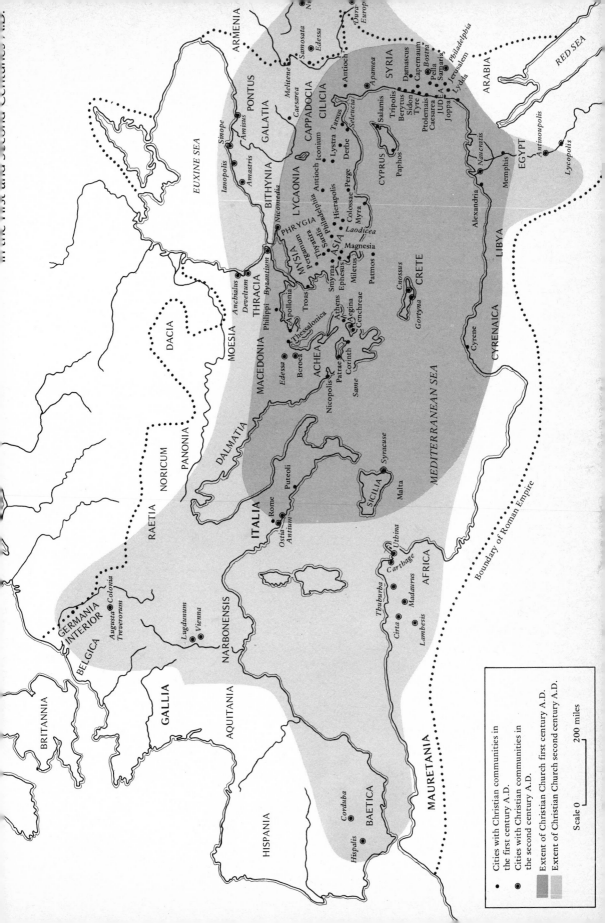

RED SEA

ARMENIA

ARABIA

Dura Europus

Samosata
Edessa

SYRIA
Antioch
Apamea
Seleucia
Damascus
Capernaum
Bostra
Pella
Samaria
Jerusalem
Philadelphia
Lydda
Joppa
JUDEA

Melitene
Caesarea

PONTUS
Sinope
Amisus
Amastris
Ianopolis

CAPPADOCIA

CILICIA
Tarsus
Salamis
Tripolis
Sidon
Tyre
Ptolemais
Berytus
Caesarea

GALATIA

CYPRUS
Paphos

EUXINE SEA

BITHYNIA
Nicomedia

LYCAONIA
Lystra
Iconium
Derbe
Antioch
Colossae
Perge
Hierapolis
Myra

Antinoupolis
Lycopolis

EGYPT

Naucratis

Memphis

Alexandria

LIBYA

PHRYGIA
Sardis
Thyatira
Philadelphia
Pergamum
Laodicea
Magnesia

MYSIA

ASIA
Smyrna
Ephesus
Miletus
Patmos

Troas
Apollonia

THRACIA
Ancbialus
Develtum
Byzantium

MOESIA

DACIA

Philippi
Thessalonica
Beroea
Edessa

MACEDONIA

ACHEA
Athens
Corinth
Aegina
Cenchreae
Patrae
Same
Nicopolis

Cnossus
Gortyna

CRETE

Cyrene

CYRENAICA

MEDITERRANEAN SEA

DALMATIA

PANONIA

NORICUM

RAETIA

Syracuse
Malta
SICILIA

Puteoli
Rome
Ostia
Antium

ITALIA

GERMANIA
INTERIOR
Augusta
Treverorum
Colonia

BELGICA

BRITANNIA

GALLIA

Lugdunum
Vienna

NARBONENSIS

AQUITANIA

HISPANIA

Corduba
Hispalis

BAETICA

MAURETANIA

AFRICA
Utbina
Carthage
Thuburba
Madaurus
Cirta
Lambesis

Boundary of Roman Empire

• Cities with Christian communities in
the first century A.D.

⊙ Cities with Christian communities in
the second century A.D.

Extent of Christian Church first century A.D.

Extent of Christian Church second century A.D.

Scale 0   200 miles

St Barnabas, missionary apostle to the Island of Cyprus, sponsor and companion of Paul. A 15th-century mural in the Church of the Holy Cross at Platanistasa, Cyprus.

Resurrection appearance of his brother. James, though not one of the original apostles, had been elected president of the Jerusalem Church and during the earliest years of the Church, when matters of policy were decided in Jerusalem, James played a vital part in the leadership of the expanding Christian Church.

It is interesting to remember that when the twelve gathered as a body to elect a substitute for Judas, the brothers of Jesus were present (Acts 1:14). James, in his capacity as chairman of the council, settled the issue of the Gentile converts with wisdom and clarity. Again, when Paul brought the poor money from the Christian congregations in the Aegean, he was received by both James and the Jerusalem elders. When Paul arrived in Jerusalem on his last and fateful visit, it was James whom he consulted and James who directed him in his attempted but unsuccessful reconciliation with the Jewish Sanhedrin. The piety of James, called 'the Just', was a by-word among Christians and Jews alike. He was meticulous in observing the

14th-century English alabaster panels, now in the Victoria and Albert Museum, show St Peter with his keys and St Paul with his sword of martyrdom.

Jewish Law and his knees were as hard as camel's knees from constant prayer and meditation.

The story of the death of James is told by Josephus. He was stoned in the Kedron Valley, after the death of the procurator Festus in the year 62 and before the arrival of the relieving procurator, Albinus. Alarmed at the rise in the number of Jewish converts to Christianity, the Sanhedrin took the opportunity to request James to denounce Jesus before the crowds, at Passover. Whether, as Josephus implies, this was a cunning priestly plan to provoke the good James into a violation of the Law, or whether James's double yoke of obedience to both the Law of Moses and of Christ misled them to expect his loyalty and co-operation, is not certainly known. What is certain is that James was made to stand up on the parapet of the temple, looking down into the Kedron ravine, and there he roundly declared his faith in the Messiahship of Jesus. 'He is now sitting in the heavens on the right hand of the Great Power, and he is about to come on the clouds of heaven.' They threw him down on to the rocks below and stoned him where a merciful fuller – beating out clothes for washing – clubbed him to death.

Such was the man whom Paul found at the head of the Christian Church and who remained so, almost until the time of Paul's own martyrdom in Rome. Under James and the 'pillars' Peter and John, the rest of the twelve – slowly declining in influence – gave the benefit of their council and teaching, at such times as they were not travelling round the Mediterranean churches. Peter, charged with the 'apostleship of the circumcision' or mission to Jews, as Paul says, visited Antioch, Corinth, Asia and ultimately Rome in the course of his duties, while John went as far as Ephesus. James, however, seems to have remained at the helm in Jerusalem and to have corresponded with Antioch and other outlying congregations by means of agents or delegates of the Jerusalem Church. These were not pioneer missionaries, but envoys, such as those who returned with Paul and Barnabas after the council in order to publish and implement its decisions. Finally the Jerusalem Church, as all the Jewish–Christian congregations, appointed its local elders who, in the style of the synagogue elders, supplied the needs of their local community. Paul's picture of the Jerusalem community is a pyramid of sometimes rather overlapping functions, from James, the 'pillars' and the twelve to the minor apostles, agents and elders. Paul's own missionary initiative and personal example rapidly brought into being a wider structure of apostolic community wherever he travelled through the Mediterranean world. Each congregation needed its elders or presbyters and each circuit of congregations required its overseer. The congregations had to keep touch with each other and their father-apostle, through agents and envoys of their own. A radical extension of the Jerusalem structure, however, came about as the missionary pioneers found themselves inevitably having to fulfil the apostolic functions of administration, preaching, pastoral supervision, and particularly of commissioning and empowering their local assistants. They found themselves having to make judgements between members of the same congregation. As the twelve were to lay their hands on the seven, and as Peter and John had done already upon the Samaritan converts, so Ananias at Damascus, if for different reasons, laid his hands upon Saul-to-become-Paul. And with exactly the same intention he said, 'the Lord hath sent me that you may be filled with the Holy Spirit'. So too, the prophets and teachers at Antioch laid their hands upon Paul and Barnabas, to commission and empower them for their first missionary venture.

The qualifications for apostleship, at the election of Matthias, had been a divinely guided selection and a constant companionship with Jesus throughout his lifetime. This would have perpetually limited the apostolate to the twelve, or at least to the seventy. How long could the apostolate be confined to a very limited number in office, rather than an unlimited number in function?

Paul boldly and passionately insisted that his own call constituted an equivalent divine selection and commission by Jesus himself, as the apostle to the Gentiles. Before Herod Agrippa, Paul declared, 'As I made my journey and drew near to Damascus, about noon a great light from heaven suddenly shone about me. And I fell to the ground and heard a voice saying to me, "Saul, Saul, why do you persecute me?" And I answered, "Who are you, Lord?" And he said to me, "I am Jesus of Nazareth whom you are persecuting." Now those who were with me saw the light but did not hear the voice of the one who was speaking to me. And I said, "What shall I do, Lord?" And the Lord said to me, "Rise, and go into Damascus, and there you will be told all that is appointed for you to do"' (Acts 22:6–10). Paul then repeated the words of Ananias's commission to him, 'The God of our fathers appointed you to know his will, to see the Just One and to hear a voice from his mouth; for you will be a witness for him to all men of what you have seen and heard' (Acts 22:14–15). Finally Paul described his direct commission when at prayer in the temple area at Jerusalem: 'I saw him [Jesus] saying to me, "Make haste and get quickly out of Jerusalem, because they will not accept your testimony about me." And I said, "Lord, they themselves know that in every synagogue I imprisoned and beat those who believed in thee." And he said to me, "Depart; for I will send you far away to the Gentiles"' (Acts 22:18, 19, 21).

Paul, confident of his true apostleship, begins several of his letters with his own testimonial. He is 'called to be an apostle, set apart for the Gospel of God' (Rom. 1:1), or 'called by the will of God to be an apostle of Jesus Christ' (1 Cor. 1), or at greater length, 'Paul an apostle – not from men nor through man, but through Jesus Christ and God the Father, who raised him from the dead' (Gal. 1:1). He insists that his apostleship is independent of the twelve, 'For I would have you know, brethren, that the gospel which was preached by me is not man's gospel. For I did not receive it from man, nor was I taught it, but it came through a revelation of Jesus Christ' (Gal. 1:11–12).

Perhaps it was Paul's example that emboldened others outside the ranks of the twelve, and even of the seventy, to claim apostleship on the score of their apostolic gifts and functions. It was natural that James, the accepted leader of the Church of Jerusalem, should have been accorded the dignity of apostleship, but such men as Barnabas and Silas earned their commission on active service. Paul claimed for such men, as for himself, 'the signs of a true apostle were performed among you in all patience, with signs and wonders and mighty works' (2 Cor. 12:12). Not all the pioneer missionaries could be accounted apostles, though all apostles were missionaries.

The later traditions that the original twelve fulfilled the missionary charge of their Master, that they divided the world between them and scattered to the corners of the earth, are suspect. They probably arose from the need of different churches to claim and defend their apostolic origin, as founded by one or more of the twelve. Eusebius may have wished to believe that 'the apostles, who were harassed in different ways with a view to destroy them and driven from the land of Judaea, had gone forth to preach the gospel to all nations, relying upon the aid of Christ. . . .'

This was said to have happened long before the Jerusalem Church left the doomed city for Pella, on the east of Jordan, in the year 66 or 67. By that time, however, the two prince-apostles, Peter and Paul, were dead, as was James the brother of Jesus. Admittedly James's successor, Simeon, a first cousin of Jesus, lived to bring back the Church to Jerusalem and to die by torture and crucifixion in the year 105, at a patriarchal age. The twelve, however, would need to have left Jerusalem soon after Pentecost to achieve a fraction of the apocryphal travels and acts attributed to them. Yet they were still in Jerusalem at the time of the Hellenist persecution in the year 36, and Luke who would gladly have described their dispersion does nothing of the kind, even though he may have written as late as the year 70 to 80.

The fact is that there is no sure and certain proof for any wider-ranging ministry of the twelve than Peter's correspondence with Asia Minor, his association with Rome, and John's link with Ephesus. Even so, neither of them are likely to have founded the churches in those cities, but rather to have built on the foundations of earlier Christian pioneers.

This need not weaken the claim of the papacy to succeed to the primacy of Peter, for Peter was primate and leader of the twelve long before he went to Rome. The fact is that the twelve were not all destined to be bishops or local church leaders. If they had been, then they would not have elected James – who was not one of them at all – to preside over the Church at Jerusalem.

It has been the custom to claim an apostolic succession, transmitted

An 1840 engraving by W. H. Bartlett of the market-place at Antioch in Syria, once the missionary headquarters of the early Christian Church.

down the centuries from those first twelve by the laying on of hands to their successors of today. This has been argued from the command to commemorate Jesus in the eucharist, the command to baptize and the statement about forgiveness. It is sometimes forgotten, however, that there is little or no evidence to show that it was the twelve alone who exercised these powers. Even the primacy of Peter does not indicate that he ever ruled without full consultation with the twelve or with his fellow apostles, nor can there be any certainty that all the bishops of the first century received any apostolic ordination from the twelve.

In the apostolic community of the first century, rather more was left to the action of the spirit of God than to the regulation of man. Similarly, the sacraments of the eucharist, of baptism and of penance would seem to have been given through the persons of the twelve, but to the *whole* apostolic community of the Church. While the twelve may have baptized, presided at the eucharist, and pronounced the forgiveness of sins, the Church must also have recognized the authority of others – like Paul and Barnabas – to do the

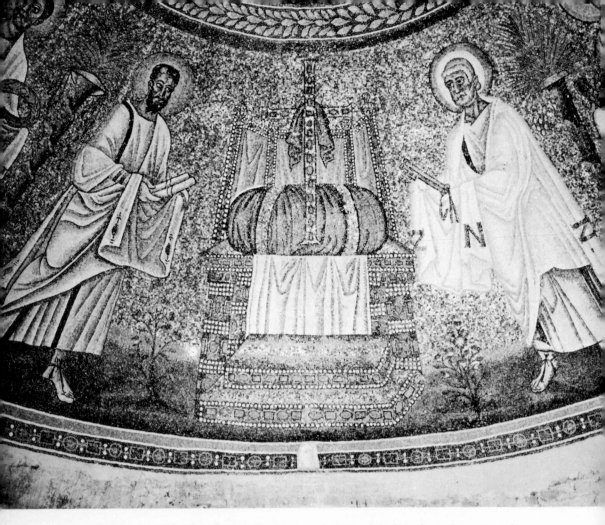

St Peter (right) and St Paul (left), prince-apostles and co-founders of the apostolic community, early portrayals on the 5th-century mosaic in the Baptistery of the Arians, at Ravenna.

same. Indeed it is the privilege of any Christian to baptize in emergency today. In the structure and function of the apostolic community, necessity has been and always will be the mother of invention.

Something of the apostolic freedom of spirit and spontaneity of affection is expressed in the words of Peter to his motley congregation of Anatolians, when he tells them, 'You are a chosen race, a royal priesthood, a holy nation, God's own people, that you may declare the wonderful deeds of him who called you out of darkness into his marvellous light' (1 Pet. 2:9).

Acknowledgements

The author and publishers gratefully acknowledge permission to quote from E. Hennecke's *New Testament Apocrypha*, edited by R. McL. Wilson, Lutterworth Press, (vol 1 1963; vol 2 1965).

Index